Literacy and Revolution

LITERACY AND REVOLUTION
The Pedagogy of Paulo Freire

Edited by Robert Mackie

Foreword by Jonathan Kozol

CONTINUUM • NEW YORK

1981
The Continuum Publishing Company
575 Lexington Avenue
New York, N.Y. 10022

Printed in the United States of America

Library of Congress Cataloging in Publication Data

Main entry under title:

Literacy and revolution, the pedagogy of Paulo
Freire.

Bibliography: p. 160
1. Literary—addresses, essays, lectures.
2. Freire, Paulo, 1921—   —addresses,
essays, lectures.
I. Mackie, Robert
LC149.L496   370'.1   81-5430

ISBN 0-8264-0055-8   AACR2

Contents

Publisher's Note

Sexism in language is a problem which radical authors are now generally aware of and avoid, but it continues to give rise to problems in two areas. The first is philosophical discourse generally, where 'man' continues to alienate 'himself' and to oppress other 'men' before (hopefully) 'he' liberates 'himself' and all 'mankind'. The second is quotation and translation. It is often argued that the text is sacred and must be quoted as it first appeared. It seems to us an open question. Sometimes the sexist modes of expression are the reason material is quoted, sometimes it is necessary to keep them because of their period flavour. But there seems no reason *on principle* to perpetuate offence just because it was once given: and in Freire's case where his ideas are genuinely non-sexist it would be doubly inappropriate to preserve linguistic forms which contradict his thought and intention.

In both cases we have altered the text where necessary with the permission of the editor.

Notes on Contributors

CLIFT BARNARD was born in England where he had wide journalistic and editorial experience before accepting a teaching post in Zambia for three years. On coming to Australia he co-founded *Radical Education Dossier*, and currently is completing research into the political economy of higher education in Nigeria.

BARBARA BEE taught for several years in English primary schools before coming to Australia where she began her own free school. Currently she teaches at Randwick Technical College in Sydney, where her principal interests lie in developing radical approaches to literacy and feminist perspectives on education.

REGINALD CONNOLLY was born in India where he taught for nearly forty years. Since coming to Australia he has completed further postgraduate study at the University of Sydney, with a thesis on the pedagogy of Paulo Freire. He recently retired from his position as a lecturer at Sydney Teachers College.

REX DAVIS worked closely for several years with Paulo Freire at the World Council of Churches in Geneva. He was the editor of *Risk*, and prior to that was involved with the Australian Council of Churches. Currently, he is canon of Lincoln Cathedral, England.

ROBERT MACKIE taught English and history in state secondary schools in NSW and lectured from 1975-77, in philosophy at Sydney Teachers' College. He now teaches at the University of Newcastle where marxist social theory and radical education comprise his main areas of activity.

MICHAEL MATTHEWS was a science teacher for some years in NSW secondary schools. After a period at Sydney Teachers College he has been, since 1975, a lecturer in philosophy of education at the University of New South Wales. He is author of *Epistemology and Education*, Harvester Books, Hassocks 1980.

JIM WALKER has lectured in philosophy of education in a variety of teachers' colleges, and at the University of Newcastle, prior to taking up his present appointment at the University of Sydney. He is co-founder of *Radical Education Dossier* and the author of a number of articles on political theory and the ideological nature of education.

Acknowledgements

On behalf of the contributors I would like to express thanks to Colin Collins, Paul Hager, Kevin Harris, Mike Kidron, Ian Lister, Bob Petersen, Rachel Sharp, Ivan Snook, Joel Spring and Lynne Turner for their helpful comments and support in the production of this book.

Robert Mackie

Foreword

by Jonathan Kozol

There are a number of increasingly disturbing ways by which a group of highly defensive North American educators attempt to undercut the relevance and value of the work of Paulo Freire and of its visible manifestations in the national literacy campaigns carried out in Guinea-Bissau and, far closer to home and therefore more alarming, in the recent Literacy Crusade of Nicaragua.

The favorite approach is to denigrate the Third World followers of Freire for having achieved "only a minimal level" of literacy in the course of their accelerated struggles towards this goal. This, say the critics, is not a degree of literacy that can be regarded as authentic, functional, or even of serious interest to a nation such as the United States.

A second approach is to attempt to caricature the work of Freire by selectively isolating particular words and phrases which distort his true intent. The tactic then is to seize upon certain passages from his early work which seem to suggest that major literacy gains can be achieved only in a setting of overt political and economic revolution. By both of these means, such critics manage to assign the impressive challenge of a broad and sophisticated body of socio-pedagogic thought to a narrow and parochial category of esoteric and impractical significance.

The first criticism can be answered best by history. In Cuba, during 1961, as later in Brazil and Chile and more recently in Nicaragua, a massive national campaign was carried out under the direct authority of scholars who identified closely with the views and practices of Dr. Freire. In the case of Cuba, the directors of the program were Abel Prieto Morales and Raúl Ferrer. Both men were consultants, enlisted by UNESCO in the spring and summer of 1980, for the Nicaraguan effort.

Cuba, like Nicaragua and like all other nations that have worked in the direct tradition of *conscientizão* [political and personal consciousness] defined most clearly in the earliest published works of Dr. Freire, endeavored at the start to achieve only a modest level of literacy: roughly comparable perhaps to what we would regard as a second/third grade level. In the Cuban situation, the mobilization made unprecedented use both of student brigadistas and of worker–volunteers who shared the actual living conditions of the illiterate campesinos [peasant/farmer] in many of the most isolated rural sections of the nation.

The success of the struggle was dramatic. From a national illiteracy rate of 24.6 percent in 1959, Cuba was able to reduce this to 5 percent in only eight months.

Far more important, and in keeping with the foresight and consistency of Freire and Ferrer, the government immediately began a sophisticated follow-up [*Seguimiento*] which led, in very short order, to a national "Battle for the Sixth Grade."

Twenty years later, Dr. Prieto was able to announce, at a conference held in Boston during January, 1981, that 1,500,000 Cubans had subsequently *achieved* that sixth grade level and that a struggle is now underway to attain a nation-wide ninth grade competence. There is every reason to believe that Nicaragua too— where Freire, Prieto and Ferrer have all contributed service as advisers to the National Crusade—will soon be able to demonstrate a comparable record of success through persistent and unwavering adaptation to the changing needs of its own social order.

The second method of attack—in charging that the ideals and practices of Freire are applicable only in a revolutionary situation— is somewhat more ingenious. Freire, after all, has told us frequently that literacy cannot be viewed in isolation from its social context, that adult education must go hand-in-hand with human liberation in the broadest sense: with health-care, land redistribution, popular participation in the process of political empowerment of the oppressed and, in general, with the radical transformation of the social system.

Freire, however, in his many dialogues on this subject with active literacy workers of our nation, has never suggested that a violent political revolution is the indisputable prerequisite to literacy work. Again and again, with painstaking effort, he has modified —*while never diluting*—his initial concept of political empowerment, in order to find an appropriate application in the context of a highly technological and politically ambiguous social system like our own.

There are, of course, all kinds of transformation, of upheaval, of "empowerment." In the context of the Third World, it is indisputable that the revolutionary fervor of a recently emancipated people has repeatedly proven to be a powerful catalyst to many essential forms of social change. One of those forms has been the total mobilization of a nation's energies in the eradication of a paralyzing situation like the nation's inability to read and write.

But there are as many other ways to introduce high motivation as there are varieties of need, of context and of prior domestication of a population. One such method is the radical North American literacy approach that has been popularized by the expression: "Dangerous Words."

The concept takes its origin in the writings of Freire concerning "generative" words—words which come from the people themselves and which, in turn, comprise the basis for a primary vocabulary—at times "a primer," at other times a number of words scratched out by literacy workers, in response to a painstaking dialogue between teacher and learner, on a chalkboard in a jungle clearing. In all cases, we are speaking of words which matter profoundly to the people and which, for just this reason, contain their own inherent catalytic power.

In keeping with the example of Freire's own work in Brazil, we would like to be concrete and understandable to those grass-roots workers who do more than meditate, argue and reflect, but who are determined to apply their words to action. What do we mean when we speak of "dangerous words" in the context of a nation such as the United States? What are examples of the kinds of words which those who toil among the urban underclass of the United States might logically expect to find emerging in the consciousness of those with whom they work?

Most certainly, we would not endeavor to invade the consciousness of the oppressed, the silent and the poor, with any predetermined list of facile and dispassionate words. We would not seek to undermine the potential indignation of those words already present in the rich and powerful oral vocabularies which exist so often in those who appear, at first, to be so broken and so meek. Nor, on the other hand, would we seek to prescribe a list of "revolutionary" words which we dogmatically decree to be appropriate to the victims of our unjust and unequal land.

Certain words, admittedly, recur with frequency in the situation of the inner-city ghetto in which this author works: not the familiar and simplistic liturgy of "Dick" and "Jane," but rather words like "grief" and "pain" and "love" and "lust" and "longing"; "lease" and "license"; "fever," "fear," "infection"; "doctor," "danger"; "fire" and "desire"; "prison," "power," "protest" and "police."

Again, we insist that these are offered as examples, not prescriptions. They represent, in one way or another, the clarification of a complex system of oppressions that may or may not, before that moment, have been present in the learner's mind. Such words will vary greatly from region to region, city to city, year to year. Those I describe are the *kinds* of words, however, which, in one particular Northeast urban context, prove time and again to grow out of the process of discussion, as learners and teachers begin to join in common efforts to achieve their goals.

Our purpose is not to encourage a radical's version of cultural imposition by arrogant prescription. Our goal is not to try to "plant" these words and concepts in the minds of those who wish to learn to read and write. The purpose, rather, is—first through the process of prior dialogue, later in the day-to-day relationship of teacher and learner—to dig down into the deep and fertile soil of those incipient concepts, dreams, longings and ideals which exist already in the consciousness of even the most broken and seemingly silent of the poor.

There is one obvious question that emerges often in discussion of the search for "generative" (or "dangerous") words in the process of literacy work in the United States. Is there perhaps an unacceptable *danger* in the use of dangerous words? On its face, this seems a naive question. In plain fact, it is a plausible concern—at least on the part of those who have the most to lose through any significant transformation of the status quo.

Might poor black people who do not have doctors, to take one vivid instance, begin to be less docile, or more "dangerous," once they learn to read and write enough to recognize the grim statistics for black infant death and black maternal death rates in the United States? Will they be "dangerous" once they possess the skills to understand the lease they sign in order to inhabit an apartment they cannot abide, for payment of a rent which they cannot afford? Will they be "dangerous" if they possess a license to drive mediocre cars out of a despairing slum into a neighborhood in which they still are not permitted to obtain a home by mortgage, or to send their kids to school?

Doctor. License. Lease. Three dangerous words.

These are the kinds of words that any serious literacy effort must be ready to hear, accept, and use, if we should hope to reach some of our concrete goals. If the ultimate goal of a North American campaign is something more substantial than the inculcation of a mechanistic and utilitarian skill, but rather the cultivation of full and humane competence and strength, awareness of rights, breadth of inquiry, ethical perseverance and persistence; if teachers hope to serve a truly liberating role; if they are striving to inspire poor people to emancipate themselves and one another from the crowded prisons of their souls, I do not see how we can obviate the possibility of danger.

To awaken people to intelligent and articulate dissent, to give voice to their longings, to give both lease and license to their rage, to empower the powerless, to give voice to those who are enslaved by their own silence—certainly this represents a certain kind of danger. It is, indeed, the type of danger which a tortured society, but one that aspires in any way at all to human justice, ought to be eager to foster, search out and encourage. If this is a danger which our social system cannot possibly afford, then we are obliged to ask ourselves if we can possibly afford this social system.

Those who insist that the ideas which proved to be of tentative success first in Brazil and Chile, later to prove triumphant in the Nicaraguan situation, would never "work" in the nonrevolutionary context of the U.S. are those who want their moment of upheaval handed to them on a silver tray. This is a perfect, and saddening, example of radical impotence bowing down before the powers of conservative self-interest.

Instead of sitting in seminar rooms at universities, praising the rebels for rebellion and the bold for their bravado, while waiting for the hour of an "ideal situation" given to us by persons or forces which we do not either dare to emulate nor strive to bring to power, it is time for North American educators to join together in a sane and viable adaptation of the work of Freire to the temporarily paralytic land in which it is our fate to live. Through the concept of literacy for personal consciousness, community autonomy and "courage to transform," we begin a process of ethical upheaval which is the only possible path to even an incipient effort at eradication of adult illiteracy within our time.

Those who hope to begin, in the United States, at the advanced and sophisticated stage of conscientization at which Freire and his earliest literacy workers finallly arrived after long years of ardor and ordeal, are doomed to the abstraction, meditation and postponement which will condemn another generation of our fellow citizens to the silence of the unempowered poor. It is our obligation to read with care the biographical data as well as the philosophic and historical reflections of the book before us, to engage with realistic aspiration (neither overly intellectual nor self-servingly abstract) in responding to the challenge that Paulo Freire has set forth. In defining that challenge, I have found the critical comradeship that pervades the long and final essay of this book—Jim Walker's "The End of Dialogue"—a particularly illuminating contribution. Walker does not indulge in the increasingly noncritical adulation of Freire-as-guru which disturbs not only his admirers but Freire himself. Happily, neither Walker not any of the other contributors to this superb collection have treated him as such; and thousands of English-speaking readers will be deeply grateful for the pungent and intelligent irreverence with which these authors state their views.

I was, for my own part, particularly intrigued by the publication here, for the first time in the United States, of a lengthy interview with Freire conducted by Rex Davis. Its appearance will provide scholars of Freire's work with some lucid clarifications, in his own words, to which few of us have yet had access. The challenge of Freire's vision is sharply focused in this interview, and the implications of that challenge culminate at length in an implicit mandate to the reader to do more than read, reflect, and engage in Freire's contemplative speculation, but *to act* in a vigorous and responsible manner on our consequent beliefs.

Of course, we do not live today in a revolutionary situation, but we do not have the right to wait for one to be presented to us. The poor cannot wait, the silent cannot wait, the conscientious teachers of this continent will refuse to wait, until the "appropriate objective conditions" are prepackaged for their use.

It is for us to create those conditions, not by adventurist rhetoric but by painstaking toil, to begin thereby the work of incremental liberation of an underclass whose servitude remains the constant framework for the all-too-comfortable and inert speculations of the uncommitted academic. We must begin, as Freire began, with piecemeal perseverance in a hostile situation. In Freire's words, "We must die as a class." But we cannot wait until the ruling members of that class are prepared to join us in an act of Christian-Marxist abnegation.

This book, several of whose authors have worked closely beside Freire for long years, is universally applicable and valuable. Its value, however, depends upon our willingness to find immediate and concrete applications.

Between Scylla and Charybdis—corporate efforts at cooption of Freire on the one hand, and an eternal justification for postponement on the other—there is a third course. It is the course of imaginative and inventive efforts to achieve what can be done in our own land and can be tried in our own time.

By any other course we will betray the man to whom this book presents a sensitive and unromantic tribute.

1. Introduction

by Robert Mackie

During recent years there has been, in many parts of the world, a considerable furore generated concerning literacy. Most often this has taken the form of assertions that the level of general literacy among schoolchildren and students in higher education has declined alarmingly. Currently in Britain, the United States, Canada and Australia, adherents to the decline and fall of literacy thesis have mounted extensive and influential campaigns to ensure that current educational practices focus more sharply on inculcating the 'three Rs'. 'Back to basics' or 'forward to fundamentals' are contemporary slogans which capture this emphasis. Moreover, such calls are often accompanied by a condemnation of teachers who, by not systematically and rigorously pursuing literacy skills, are accused of failing to provide students with an adequate preparation either for post-school education or work. Alleged deficiencies in literacy are then explicitly linked, particularly in the countries mentioned, with high rates of unemployment among young people.

On closer examination however, there is much in this argument that is naive and simplistic. Underlying it is a conception of literacy as the mere technique of reading and writing, which can be simply imparted, simply absorbed, and simply utilised. Viewed in this light, literacy is achieved when mechanical skills are acquired. Yet there is far more to it than this. What is especially ignored is the understanding that literacy is a process which continues throughout life. To be literate is not to have arrived at some pre-determined destination, but to utilise reading, writing and speaking skills so that our understanding of the world is progressively enlarged. Furthermore, literacy is not acquired neutrally, but in specific historical, social and cultural contexts. Far from being an end which merely reflects reality, as many current literacy iconoclasts imply, it is the means by which

1

we comprehend, unravel and transform the reality in which we find ourselves. Indeed, the glaring omission in most functional analyses of literacy lies precisely in the failure to examine the context in which literacy actually functions. Thus literacy comes to be portrayed, in abstract and reified terms, as something which exists in a vacuum, remote and removed from other social relations. The same intellectual sleight of hand is at work when the inability of youth to gain employment is correlated with deficiencies in teaching. Few of the participants in this somewhat overheated debate go beyond the how of literacy, and explore the more fundamental questions of what, where, and why we read, write and speak the way we do.

One contemporary educator who neither ignores the means nor confuses the ends of literacy is the Brazilian Paulo Freire. Not only does he provide a viable, effective method for teaching adult illiterates; he also states, with admirable clarity and force, the inherently political nature of literacy. Strongly opposing the myths of neutrality, objectivity and impartiality which percolate every facet of education, Freire convincingly demonstrates that literacy can serve either to liberate human beings or domesticate them. His choice – and indeed that of every humanist educator – is, and must be the former.

Paulo Freire's essential contribution lies in his recognition of the way language forms our perceptions of the world, and our intentions towards it. In doing so he highlights the connections between language, politics and consciousness. Conceiving the task of literacy to be humanisation, Freire is led inevitably to an examination of the ways social and political structures impede this goal. As a consequence, his discussion of literacy and education has as one of its principal concerns the promotion of revolutionary social change. Freire's pedagogy focuses on human liberation from oppression, not only in Brazil, but everywhere oppression exists. So, while his theory has situated origins, its applications are potentially much wider. Consistent with the very best of educational traditions, Freire's ideas derive from practice, are moulded into theoretical explanations and perspectives, returning once again to be refurbished in practice. Eschewing both mindless activity and empty, recondite theorising, Freire unites action with reflection. The resultant praxis provides his work with a vital dynamic whereby literacy and education come to be seen as fully political constructs.

Paulo Freire: A Brief Biography[1]

Freire was born in 1921 in the town of Recife, situated on the Atlantic seaboard coast at the most eastern point of the South American continent. His family was middle class, and although his mother was a devout catholic his father was not. The religious differences between his parents apparently did not produce conflict or tension in the household since each parent respected the other's position. Freire's early childhood corresponded with the years of worldwide economic depression and his family, like so many others, experienced hunger and poverty. Even though malnutrition caused him to fall behind at school, Freire remembers how the outward symbols of social class separated him from the other children. The fact that his father continued to wear a tie, and that his house contained a German piano, signified to others distinctions of class that could not be erased. As Freire says, 'we shared the hunger, but not the class'. By the time his brothers were old enough to work the family's position had improved. Freire was able to complete high school successfully, and proceeded to Recife University where he studied to be a teacher of Portuguese.

In 1944 Freire met his wife Elza, who was also a teacher. Together they shared a career in teaching, and began to work as well in the 'catholic action' movement, among other middle-class families in Recife. Freire recalls that this involved trying to explain the contradiction between the demands of christian faith and petit-bourgeois lifestyles. It proved to be an extremely disheartening experience, as they uncovered strong resistance to the idea that bourgeois families should, for example, treat their servants as human beings. 'After this', Freire comments, 'we started to make our choices. We decided not to keep working with the bourgeois, and instead to work with the people.'

This shift in the direction of their lives was not accomplished however, without many mistakes. Freire recounts one occasion where he talked with the workers about the psychologist Jean Piaget: 'I said many beautiful things, but made no

3

impact. This was because I used my frame of reference, not theirs.' After his speech finished one worker said to Freire, 'You talk from a background of food, comfort and rest. The reality is that we have one room, no food, and have to make love in front of the children.' Freire reports that at this time he could not understand such reactions. It was only from a continual and prolonged process of both research and living with the poor in the slums of Recife that he finally understood the syntax of the people. 'I was not a myth in those days', he says, 'and I had more time'. Freire's endeavours in this area provided the framework for his doctoral thesis on the teaching of adult illiterates, which was submitted to Recife University in 1959. Not long after, the university appointed him to a chair in the history and philosophy of education.

In 1962 Miguel Arraes, mayor of Recife, sponsored a programme to promote adult literacy in the municipality, and appointed Paulo Freire as its co-ordinator. It was in this context that the famous 'culture circles' were launched. So pronounced was Freire's success in Recife that in the following year the government of President Joao Goulart invited him to become Director of the National Literacy Programme. Thus Freire's influence extended out from Recife to encompass the entire country. In his new post Freire hoped to parallel the dramatic results of Fidel Castro's campaign during 1960-64 to eliminate illiteracy in Cuba. With the support of Education Ministers Paulo de Tarso and Julio Sambaquy, Freire drew up plans to import 35,000 Polish slide projectors and establish 20,000 'culture circles' throughout Brazil. Eight-month training courses were begun for co-ordinators in nearly every state. It was anticipated that by 1964 two million people would be undergoing Freireian literacy programmes.

Not all sections of Brazilian society, however, viewed these developments with enthusiasm. The conservative Rio de Janeiro paper, *O Globo*, charged that the Freire method was stirring up the people, giving them ideas about changing things, and hence fomenting subversion. Responding to accusations that he was intending to 'Bolshevise the country', Freire notes that his actual crime was to treat literacy as more than a mechanical problem. By linking literacy to critical consciousness it became an effort to liberate the people, and not simply an instrument to dominate them. Although the political climate was favourable, the Freireian programme was given little time to demonstrate its full effectiveness. As events turned out Freire had less than eighteen months.

On 1 April 1964 the Goulart government was deposed by the military in a coup d'etat. The army has held power ever since, and one of the original perpetrators, Joao Figueiredo, is the current president. While the coup had many causes, none was perhaps more fundamental than the fear among the upper and middle classes that the country was undergoing a major shift of power. Under Brazil's constitution illiterates were forbidden to vote, so the extension of literacy carried in its wake a growing democratisation of the country. In the eyes of the military, and other powerful sections of Brazilian society, this constituted a threat to the political monopoly enjoyed by the few.

As both a professor at Recife University, and as national head of the literacy programme, Paulo Freire was an eminent, influential, and to some, a highly dangerous figure. Soon after the coup he was arrested, expelled from his university post, and jailed for seventy-five days. He was vilified as an enemy of God and the Americans. After protracted negotiations, Freire was eventually granted political asylum in Bolivia. Unfortunately this respite proved short-lived, for fifteen days later Bolivia itself experienced a coup. Once more Freire left and late in 1964 arrived in Chile, where he was to stay for five years.

In Chile the government of President Eduardo Frei regarded the problem of adult illiteracy as serious enough to warrant the creation, in mid-1965, of a Department of Special Planning for the Education of Adults. Its director was Waldemar Cortes, principal of a night school in Santiago. Cortes made contact with Freire, who had been given a position at the University of Chile, and decided to implement his literacy method. This raised the immediate problem of gaining acceptance in Chile for a method considered subversive in Brazil. A number of people in the governing Christian Democrat party considered Freire to be radical, even communist. With persuasion and effort however, Cortes managed to get the programme accepted. In this way Freire became involved in the Chilean Agrarian Reform Corporation, particularly its training and

5

research institute, which put the adult literacy programme into practice on behalf of Cortes' department.

Freire's period in Chile was especially fruitful in other ways as well. During this time he wrote up his Brazilian experience in the monograph *Education: the Practice of Freedom*, which was published in Rio in 1967, with an introduction contributed by his colleague Francisco Weffort. Two years later Freire's examination of the problems of agrarian reform, *Extension or Communication*, was published in Santiago, accompanied by a preface from the leading Chilean economist Jacques Chonchol. It was, however, another five years before these works appeared in English under the title *Education for Critical Consciousness.*[2] Preceding this, so far as English readers were concerned, was the translation of Freire's most important book, *Pedagogy of the Oppressed*. This was completed in 1968 and appeared as Freire's first work in English two years later.

In 1969 he accepted an invitation to be a visiting professor for the following year at Harvard University's Centre for Studies in Education and Development. Thus Freire left Chile before Salvador Allende's marxist government was elected to power in 1970, and he returned only briefly during Allende's period of office. Nonetheless, it is significant to note that when Allende was violently overthrown in 1973 the regime of General Pinochet lost little time in declaring Freire *persona non grata*.

Freire's year at Harvard was a notable personal success as his ideas found a large and sympathetic audience in North America. During 1970 he wrote a series of articles for the *Harvard Educational Review* on adult literacy and 'conscientisation'. These were immediately published by that journal as a monograph under the title *Cultural Action for Freedom*. Two years later they were re-issued under the same title by Penguin Books in Britain. The opportunity to work in North America also brought Freire into contact with other radical critics of education, particularly Jonathan Kozol and Ivan Illich. Freire participated in a series of seminars with Illich at the Centre for Intercultural Documentation in Cuernavaca during the summers of 1969 and 1970. Initially Freire and Illich enjoyed a close personal friendship, but this has noticeably waned in recent years as their interests, activities, and perspectives have increasingly diverged.[3]

Freire left Harvard in 1970 to take up his current appointment as special consultant to the Office of Education at the World Council of Churches in Geneva. This has further enlarged the scope of his influence and practical involvement in education, especially in Africa. In the decade and a half since his exile from Brazil, Freire has worked in Peru, Angola, Mozambique, Tanzania, and Guinea-Bisseau. In addition he has participated in seminars and symposia in Canada, the USA, Italy, Iran, India, Australia and Papua-New Guinea. Recognition of Freire's contribution to education was paid in 1973 by the Open University in Britain, which awarded him an honorary doctorate. The following year he went to Australia, under the sponsorship of the Australian Council of Churches, to take part in a conference on 'Education for Liberation and Community'.

As part of his work in Geneva, Freire established the Institute of Cultural Action in 1971. This is an endeavour, through research and experimentation, to establish a political pedagogy based on conscientisation. Over the last few years the Institute has produced a series of documents focusing on the liberation of women, political education in Peru, and the contradictions underlying aid programmes for the third world. One of its recent publications highlights Freire's current work in Guinea-Bissau. Indeed since 1975 Freire has become deeply involved in designing an educational process appropriate to the demands facing that newly independent country. An account of his activities in Guinea-Bissau was published in 1978 under the title *Pedagogy in Process: The Letters to Guinea-Bissau.*[4] In many ways this is the most readable and accessible of Freire's books. What emerges clearly is that he has found the context of West Africa quite different to that of Brazil. So the adult literacy programmes for Guinea-Bissau have not simply been transplanted from Brazil, but reinvented within the particular cultural milieu of post-colonial Africa. This work has reinvigorated his thinking and brought him once again into close practical contact with the problems of adult literacy and education.

Moreover, late in 1979, there were some indications that Freire's long period of exile from Brazil may soon be over. In

7

September of that year President Figueiredo granted amnesties to some five thousand Brazilian exiles and dissidents, including Miguel Arraes and Paulo Freire. This enabled Freire to make a return to his homeland for the first time in fifteen years. While it may be a little premature at this stage to forecast a permanent resettlement for Freire in Brazil, there can be little doubt that his future – whether in Geneva, Africa or South America – will continue to be dominated by a longstanding commitment to the struggle for liberation. In effect, his life, work and thought can be succinctly expressed in the Portuguese phrase *viver e lutar* – to live is to struggle.

On Understanding Paul Freire

Freire's work has taken some considerable time to become widely known in the English speaking world, where reactions to him have been many and varied. Broadly, they could be categorised as falling into four groups. By far the largest and most enthusiastic are those who write from a religious perspective similar to that of Freire himself. Indeed conscientisation has become a commonly employed term in the rhetoric of many church-based aid agencies. Discussion of Freire's views occupies many pages in ecumenical journals like *Convergence* and its Australian counterpart *Dialogue.* What unites such accounts is the determination to cast Freire's work within an idealist framework where the motivation for his radical educational proposals can be found in what is called the 'theology of liberation'. Nor should adulation from this quarter be surprising when one considers Freire's religious involvements both in Brazil and with the World Council of Churches. Perhaps the most representative discussions of Freire from this perspective can be found in the articles by Bruce Boston,[5] Clift Wright,[6] and in the book *Conscientisation and Deschooling* (1974) by John Elias.[7]

The second group, though lesser in number, were also early into the field of Freire interpretation. These are the adult educators who can be found in a collection edited by Stanley M. Grabowski, *Paulo Freire: A Revolutionary Dilemma for the Adult Educator* (1972).[8] The writers consider the political questions posed by Freire, and wrestle with ways to denude, domesticate, absorb and eventually nullify the challenge he makes to their functionalism. Not only do they collectively fail to understand Freire's politics, some even question whether education is a political event at all. For these people Freire has written in vain. The only redeeming feature of the Grabowski collection is its extensive bibliography, gathered with all the awesome efficiency computer technology can offer to the modern academic.

It is unfortunate, and perhaps revealing, that only a handful of authors have concerned themselves with one of the central components of Freire's work – namely his theory of literacy. Literacists like Herbert Kohl, Cynthia Brown,[9] the Swedes Carol and Lars Berggren,[10] and the English writer Martin Hoyles[11] have penetrated Freire's methodology and glimpsed something of its wider social ramifications. In spite of this however, literacist interpreters of Freire are often hampered by an ethnocentric view of his methodology in relation to English speaking cultures. This weakness is augmented by the tendency to accept Freire's method as a recipe ready made and directly applicable. This overlooks the necessity, stressed by Freire, to rework and remould his pedagogical suggestions in a manner consonant with the history of particular social formations. Failure here guarantees that his vital contribution to this area will meet with limited understanding.

The fourth group of Freire critics are perhaps the most interesting, if not always the most enlightening. These are those who take issue more or less directly with the political impetus of his pedagogy. Within this group we find sophisticated conservatives like Peter Berger, whose *Pyramids of Sacrifice* (1974)[12] contains a chapter accusing Freire of condescension and elitism in his relations with the oppressed. For Berger conscientisation is not critical consciousness but consciousness raising – a misunderstanding which results in a serious misreading of Freire. From a very different perspective Joel Spring's *A Primer of Libertarian Education* (1975)[13] recognises the dialectic of thought and action which lies at the core of Freire's praxis. Yet he conceives this largely in individualist rather than class terms, and so the possibilities for mutuality and solidarity are passed over. In a similar vein, Denis Gleeson writing on 'Theory and Practice in the Sociology of Paulo Freire' (1974)[14] correctly identifies the

9

unity of theory and practice in Freire while suggesting at the same time that his politics are, of all things, Jeffersonian.

Confronted by this kaleidoscope of misinformation, misrepresentation and downright nonsense concerning Freire, the time for a penetrating, constructive and critical explication of his work has surely arrived. The essays which follow seek to achieve this by bringing Freire's politics firmly to the fore. Moreover, our intention here is to treat his work historically by tracing both its origins in north-east Brazil and its subsequent development in Africa. An essential starting point to this task is an adequate exploration of the political economy of Brazilian education. In the following chapter Clift Barnard's analysis provides this framework and indicates not only why imperialism has been a recurrent spectre over Brazilian politics, but also why culture circles were the appropriate pedagogic form for Pernambuco's poor.

Barbara Bee continues this theme by developing the thesis that literacy teaching is infused with political considerations. She contends it can be either liberating or repressive, and argues forcefully for the recognition of this in opposition to prevailing functionalist approaches. That such opposition is central to Freire's method is made clear in the following chapter, which is the text of an interview Freire gave to *Risk* editor Rex Davis. Here we see something of the way Freire formulates his practice and the connections it has with his wider educational and political concerns.

Reginald Connolly takes these further in chapter five by examining the interdependent unity of Freire's theory and practice. Connolly focuses on the political nature of teaching and suggests ways in which Freireian teachers could proceed to advance the goal of humanisation.

Underlying all educational proposals is some theory of knowledge, or epistemology. And in many respects Freire's contribution here, as Michael Matthews explains, represents one of the few attempts to elaborate the pedagogy implicit in Marx's *Theses on Feuerbach*. Matthews contends that Freire's epistemology is motivated by a concern to make socially productive individuals subjects in the act of knowing so they can intervene in and transform their world. As such it becomes a focus for examining the connections between knowledge, action and power.

The final two chapters are an attempt to enter fully into a debate with Freire's theory – especially its origins and outcomes. By delineating some of the manifold contributions to his thought I hope to have made a little clearer his intellectual roots and context, while at the same time raising questions about the overall coherence of his work. These latter problems are analysed by Jim Walker in his rigorously critical examination of Freire's political theory and practice. By focusing on Guinea-Bissau Walker places Freire's recent work under close scrutiny, and argues that there are serious contradictions and incoherencies embedded in his political stance.

While recognising that Freire's work is far from faultless, the essays presented here nonetheless affirm that his theory is of prime importance for all those engaged in political struggles for education. It is to advance such struggles that these essays have been written.

2. Imperialism, Underdevelopment and Education
Clift Barnard

> In Latin America historically the education and social systems have worked together to deny citizens both the competencies and opportunities for significant participation, the basic means for affecting social change. . . . This is the result of the conscious and wilful manipulation of existing institutional power . . . by social elites to maintain the status quo.[1]

To study Paulo Freire is to reflect on liberation. The themes which inform his writing – oppression, dialogue, cultural action – reveal a sharp sense of the conflicts in the human condition. Suffering and struggle have dominated his own life. As a young man he experienced hunger, as a political exile he has known the helpless fury of seeing his work destroyed by uniformed barbarians in the name of christian civilisation. At the same time, the hardship and disappointment of a long exiled scholar are trivial in comparison with the misery of millions of Latin Americans, for whom poverty and political oppression are routine. To the peasant submerged in the daily business of survival, often not consciously aware of oppression and exploitation since they are synonymous with living, freedom has no meaning because the unknown cannot be thought about. Freire has spent his life helping people to find a meaning for freedom by giving them the tools to name the world – that is, to become conscious of their own oppression and therefore seize the opportunity to change it.

Yet educators the world over have thought that they could improve human welfare if only there were more education. In what way is Freire different from others who have tried? And what does the larger-than-life technicolor melodrama of Latin America have to do with more stable, secure environments? The

12

first of these questions is discussed in other chapters of this book. My task is to explain the background from which Freire comes, and in doing so to show that the suffering of which Freire speaks is not something 'out there', unrelated to events nearer home. It is the historical product of colonial expansion, serving the needs of an increasingly integrated global economic and political system. Initiatives in one sector will produce effects elsewhere. The poverty of the Brazilian peasant, in other words, is as much a part of the western way of life as the pollution and street crime which choke our cities.

To understand this is to come to terms with some of Freire's central themes, notably his insistence that education is always political, and that the aim of good pedagogy is to enable people to increase their understanding of their own objective conditions. Such understanding, says Freire, will inevitably lead them to change the world as they climb out of the oppression in which they have been submerged. The major task of western educators, then, should be to describe the political function of education in capitalist societies, unmasking its operation as an instrument of class oppression. As they do this, the relevance of Freire's writing for societies everywhere will become apparent.

In examining the process of Brazilian underdevelopment, we shall consider briefly the economic history of the country, review the conditions of the north-eastern part of the country where Freire set up his literacy programme, and discuss the political events directly related to Freire's work. This will include an analysis of the role of education in the recent history of Brazil. Some of the implications of the Brazilian development strategy will come out of that discussion.

Historical Background to Brazilian Underdevelopment

The European 'discovery' of Brazil was by a Portuguese explorer, Pedro Alvares Cabral, in 1500. It remained under the Portuguese monarchy until independence in 1822. The colonial society which emerged during those three centuries was defined at first by the structure of Portuguese society itself, and left behind it a legacy which determined the manner of Brazil's integration into the modern imperial economy.

13

In the early sixteenth century, Iberia was isolated from many of the renaissance influences affecting the rest of Europe. The struggle against Islam, and the mountain barriers which separated the peninsula from France, contributed to a slower transition from feudalism to capitalism than took place elsewhere. Urbanisation was less rapid than in other countries, the population more scattered, and the bourgeoisie less powerful in relation to the traditional landowning classes. With a population of about one million, Portugal ranked lower down the colonial scale than England, France or even Holland. Because of the weakness of the bourgeoisie, and the lower level of capital accumulation available, the colonial movement into Brazil retained some feudal characteristics. The limitations of the metropolitan power had far-reaching consequences for the type of economy which emerged.

The first phase of penetration was confined mainly to trade with the Indians and the extraction of native dyewoods, among them the Brazilwood from which the country takes its name. Later the Portuguese granted vast tracts of land for settlement, mainly to the impoverished feudal nobility anxious to recoup fortune in the new world. The means by which they succeeded initially in establishing themselves can be summed up in one word: sugar. The huge areas of land handed over by the crown to *donatarios* were subdivided into *sesmarias*, themselves enormous units of plantation size, still too large to allow the growth of a small farmer class or self-employed artisans.

The realisation that the rich, black *massape* soil of the north-east coast was ideal for growing sugar cane set the pattern for commercial monoculture which was followed, to a greater or lesser extent, as the new crop was developed in each region. In the second half of the sixteenth century, Portugal built up a virtual monopoly in international sugar production, based on slave labour organised in *latifundia* (plantations) ruled by an aristocracy whose power over the slaves was virtually absolute. Sugar was produced for the external market, and manufactured goods bought from the metropolitan power, which in turn took steps to prevent the growth of Brazilian industries that might compete with Portuguese ones.

Thus the characteristic economic structure was set from the

14

earliest times: an export-oriented cash-crop sector provided the ruling elite with the income it needed to buy its manufactured goods from abroad. Sugar itself declined in importance to the Brazilian economy during the seventeenth century. For a time there was stagnation, until new products such as gold, timber and rubber began to be exploited and then declined in turn.

Portugal controlled the Brazilian export-import trade until the early nineteenth century, though not the more profitable distribution of sugar once it had been brought across the sea. During the nineteenth century, control of the export-import trade slipped out of Portuguese hands to be taken over by Britain, and the role of metropolitan power, buying up raw materials and selling manufactures, was increasingly filled by Britain as the leading imperial nation of the day. The domestic economy continued much as before, except that coffee grown in the central-southern region around Sao Paulo had become far and away the most important crop, making up nearly half of the country's exports by the mid-nineteenth century. Large estates, slave labour and low capitalisation were still the salient features of the economic struggle. There was little or no attempt to industrialise or develop a domestic market. 'The immense influx of funds brought to the country by the coffee industry served no purpose save for the purchase of British manufactured goods.'[2] Throughout the period of the Empire, from independence to the founding of the Republic in 1889, Brazil was in a chronic financial crisis, despite the massive expansion of its exports. The opposition of the landowners to taxes on exports, and the opposition of the British to levies on imports, meant that state expenditure had to be met from borrowing. Control of credit by the British-owned banks stifled new industry, and so those enterprises which did start soon passed under foreign control.

However, the one advantage possessed by Brazil was local ownership of the land. This eventually enabled local accumulation of capital to take place, giving some scope for industrialisation. Social and political changes analogous to those taking place in Europe occurred in Brazil in tandem with the beginnings of industrialisation. The urban middle class grew in numbers and political strength, and enjoyed some support from the military for a liberal-nationalist thrust which led to the abolition of

15

slavery in 1888, and a year later to the establishment of the Republic. The Republican regime made determined efforts to set up local industries and encourage immigration at a rate in excess of 100,000 a year up to the turn of the century. The addition of more than a million people, many of them with some money and vocational skills, spurred the development of new enterprises. At the same time, the constant devaluation of the currency, demanded by the coffee-growers to boost their exports, made imported manufacturers more expensive and helped local entre-preneurs to get started. By the end of the nineteenth century the composition of imports had become much less primitive, and the significant imports – coal, tools, machines – were themselves generating industrial growth. From time to time, the metropoli-tan powers were able to discourage this process, but major dislocations of the western economy, such as the two world wars and the depressions of the 1890s and 1930s, gave a fillip to Brazil's import-substitution, on which its industrialisation was based. The collapse of the coffee market with the depression of 1930, for example, meant a virtual cessation of income and investment from abroad for several years, so that hitherto foreign-dominated markets were opened up to domestic manu-facturers. Industrial production doubled between 1931 and 1938. Government assistance in the form of tariffs and infrastructure development assisted the process.

After the second world war, the pattern began to change. The model of growth through import-substitution to satisfy consumer demand had been built on a very small part of the population. The vast mass of peasants – still fifty per cent of the nation – remained virtually excluded from the consumption. Urban and industrial workers, though much better off than the peasants, were unable to provide as big a market as the capacity of industry required. In short, a consumer economy could not flourish in a society where some equalisation of incomes and a reasonable measure of social justice did not exist, and bottle-necks began to be apparent. Meanwhile, direct North American investment had become an important element in the economy. Nearly $1,100,000,000 flowed in between 1951 and 1960, setting up industries inside the tariff barriers but in fact subject to US control.

As industrial production moved from the centre to the periphery, the relations of production that had characterised the old system were not overthrown, they were extended. Instead of being connected to the centre primarily in terms of the exchange of commodities, the periphery became part of an integrated system of industrial production whose ownership continued to remain in substantial measure in the centre. The obverse side of industrialisation on the periphery was the insertion of foreign-owned enterprise squarely in the middle of the industrial order that was created. Imperialism, in short, was internalised.[3]

The restricted size of the market placed limits on import-substitution in consumer durables. This sector had, however, a large measure of Brazilian ownership. The big area still dominated by imports was the heavy capital goods sector. Direct US investment went some way towards reducing capital goods imports, while growing exports of manufactured goods helped to bypass the limitations of the domestic market. In this way the ruling elite was able to avoid the social change necessary to develop domestic consumption, at the same time as it integrated Brazil into a global production system dominated by trans-national companies. The price for the elite was increased dependence on centres of power outside their control, together with chronic inflation, but the payoff was continued growth without an extension of participation in the political process, with all the dangers and 'instability' that would have entailed. The consequence was the classic problem of third world countries – growth without development, where development is defined as an improvement in *general* welfare. The Brazilian economic miracle was to a large extent the result of increased output per worker rather than increased employment or higher wages. Twenty million people were added to the workforce from the twenties to the sixties, but only one-sixth of them went into manufacturing industry. A third went into agriculture and the rest into services. During the sixties, income distribution became still more unequal. The share of national income going to the poorest 40 per cent of the population fell from 11.2 per cent in

17

1960 to 9 per cent in 1970; that of the top 5 per cent rose from 27.4 per cent to 36.3 per cent in the same period.

From classic colonial dependency, through an uneasy nationalist alliance of the so-called 'feudal' aristocracy with the new urban capitalists, to 'associated-dependent' absorption in the international capitalist division of labour – this has been the evolution of Brazil's underdevelopment. When we speak of underdevelopment, we do not mean some primal state of pre-industrial poverty, in which isolated backward territories some-how miss out on the wealth of advanced capitalist countries. We are talking about a condition which the rich in rich countries have induced in the poor, and in which a global system marginalises ever-larger numbers of people in the search for profit. The cost of this in resource use is something with which the western world is struggling to come to terms, seeing limits to its own growth. The cost in human misery is not yet fully perceived by many in advanced capitalist societies. The myth persists that more capitalist growth can still solve the problems of Latin America, Asia and Africa, despite the fact that Latin America has now had capitalist penetration for nearly five centuries and is still underdeveloped. Let us now look in more detail at the price paid by the people of Brazil for the wealth advanced capitalist countries enjoy, and consider some of the implications of the growth ideology.

Poverty in the North-east

The north-east of Brazil is one of the most wretched regions on earth. Despite the abolition of slavery in 1888, the social formation remains strongly hierarchical: a mass of largely illiterate, landless labourers work for a small class of wealthy landowners in conditions of misery and poverty that defy description.

The north-east region covers six hundred thousand square kilometres spread over seven states, and has a population of about thirty million. Writing in the *New York Times* in 1960 (around the time Freire was active there), Tad Szulc described some of the conditions: seventy-five per cent illiteracy (the national average: less than fifty per cent); a life expectancy of twenty-eight for men and thirty-two for women; a birth rate of two and a half per cent per year, but with gastric diseases wiping out vast numbers of babies. Incidentally, concern in the United States at this time centred not so much on the humanitarian issue of suffering as on the success of the Cuban revolution and the fear that the rest of Latin America would 'go communist'.

How is it that such a situation can continue for so long? Why have the people of the north-east allowed themselves to be denied a share of the wealth their labour has produced? In a graphic account of the region, Josue de Castro argues that they

> have been slow to develop into a social entity, and they have only sporadic and limited experience of common aspirations. The struggle for survival has left them little scope for social action. Meanwhile, battening down this dumbly suffering mass is a ruling establishment made up of people who are spiritually and socially abortive.[4]

Geographically, the north-east can be divided into two basic areas, and an intermediate zone: one area is the lush, fertile coastal strip where the sugar is grown; the other is the dry hinterland of the *sertao*, where life has always been harsh and where it is periodically made impossible by droughts which decimate livestock and reduce the people to starving refugees – *retirantes*. The starvation and poverty however, are social rather than geographical. The exclusive devotion to sugar led the landowners to destroy the natural forest and wildlife of the coastal areas almost completely, so that the diet of the plantation workers was impoverished, often consisting largely of manioc, a tuber which grows easily but is low on nutritional value. Since sugar growing demanded increasing amounts of land, food cultivation was forced onto more and more marginal soil, closer to the *sertao*. And in a conflict over whether to grow sugar for export or food for the workers, the outcome was rarely in doubt. Figures on land tenure throw some light on this: in 1956, twenty per cent of the rural inhabitants owned land; the other eighty per cent were rentiers, sharecroppers and the like. Half of the land in the north-east was owned by three per cent of the population. Partly as a result, per capita income in the north-east was only forty per cent of the national average.

19

The landless masses were viewed like the oxen at the mills, as two-legged animals to be yoked to the heavy feudal cart. They were marginal and faceless, denied the least means of access to the rights and privileges of their overlords.[5]

Chronic undercultivation is also a factor in this cycle of poverty. When a landowner cannot sell cash crops on the local or international markets, profits cannot be made and so the land is left idle, regardless of human need. So it was that in 1950, of the 125 million acres of agricultural holdings, only one-tenth was cultivated.

To maintain the peasants in their servitude, the landowning class developed a set of institutions designed to keep their workers poor, however hard they might work. Retrograde rents, payment in kind or through work for the landlord, control of retail outlets through which peasants spent their income, control of credit and other measures kept a tight rein on the lower orders.

> These institutions, peculiar to the large Brazilian estates, have been likened by some specialists in Brazilian affairs to feudal or semifeudal institutions. The comparison is false. They came into being after the abolition of slavery and still exist today. Their specific purpose is greater profit margin . . . Clearly they are capitalist institutions fallen into decay under conditions of extreme underdevelopment.[6]

The system of land tenure on the *latifundia* made it virtually impossible for anything resembling a middle class to grow up between the impoverished and the wealthy. In the hinterland, large cattle ranches were developed, initially for hides and later to feed the people of the mining areas of Minas Gerais to the south. Here ownership was more diverse and economic links with other parts of the country more extensive. But with the lack of local development – for instance, in the form of water storage and irrigation systems designed to help the peasants survive during drought – the people were entirely exposed to disaster when drought did come, as it inevitably did every few years. The inhabitants of the *sertao* would be forced to flee, straggling down the roads to the coastal cities and towards the south. Many would die of thirst and starvation on the way; more would die when the rains came, and with them infectious diseases, stimulated by the people's weakened resistance. In the drought of 1877, the provincial capital of Fortaleza had 80,000 cases of smallpox in its population of 124,000. Nearly 54,000 deaths were recorded from smallpox, beri beri, yellow fever, and other diseases. In some places, the death toll was fifty per cent of the population.

> The vested interests did their best to make periodic drought the scapegoat of the north-east, but in reality not all of the north-east is dry, and drought is by no means the basic cause of all calamity, even in the deep *sertao*. However, it took time to prove this and then to convince public opinion in other parts of the country that underdevelopment and starvation in the north-east were mainly due to social and economic inequalities, not to scanty rainfall.[7]

Those who fled permanently from the drought were destined to become shanty-dwellers on the fringes of coastal cities like Recife, or to migrate as unskilled labour to the growing industries of the centre-south. Indeed, the greater economic openness of the *sertao* was a factor in the growth of a different facet of Brazilian underdevelopment – internal colonialism. This is a process, analogous to that of international colonialism, in which capital and workers flow from backward to metropolitan regions within one country. The migration of workers to the South African gold reef is similar.

During the nineteenth century, with the relative decline in the importance of sugar, many of the aristocracy of the north-east invested in coffee or in new industrial enterprises, causing an outflow of capital from what was now a peripheral area to the economic centre. Alliances were formed between some of the traditional landowners and new entrepreneurs (often they were the same people anyway), so that the relationship of under-developed primary producer to dominant manufacturer which characterised Brazil's links with Europe and North America, was reflected within the country itself. The more efficient land-use in the south – more intensive production on small properties, often owned by the farmers who worked them, rather than by absentee landlords – coupled with freer immigrant settlement and the

21

closeness of markets, allowed a more vigorous and differentiated economy to come into being than had been known in the north-east, though the two were not entirely separate and ownership links were important.

So, far from disseminating prosperity to all classes and regions in the country, industrial growth on the capitalist model drained the backward areas still further, siphoning the surplus from those areas for investment where profits were higher, and driving people off the land and into marginal petty services or industrial sweated labour. In the long-term historical perspective, this movement may be seen as being as progressive as the shift from feudalism to capitalism. But its impact on the social fabric of the north-east was to aggravate an already hideous environment.

> Drought and famine are natural hazards in most of the backlands. This is unavoidable. But when the given hazards of the *sertao* are reinforced by a merciless social and economic system, the pain becomes intolerable. Ill-times and sporadic local rebellions . . . are not merely incidental historical events, as many think, they are a very significant expression of the feudalistic mould of Brazil's colonial history. The banditry that from time to time terrorised the region, as well as the epidemics of mystic delirium and destructive hatred, were nothing but dis-ordered and unco-ordinated expressions of a latent urge to revolt by a population fenced in like cattle in a pasture without grass.[8]

Eventually, resistance did begin to coalesce. The historic bandits – the *cangaceiros* – whose Robin Hood adventures won them the admiration of the people, were isolated and easily defeated. Their image, significantly, was a criminal one. For the illiterate masses, lacking in social organisation or political awareness, an improvement in living standards was little or more than a remote dream. For their rulers, needless to say, it was inconceivable that such an improvement could ever be legitim-ate. Political and cultural movements of this sort were by definition 'subversive'. To understand the political context in which Freire and other educational movements in the north-east were operating, it is now necessary to review rapidly the recent political history of Brazil.

From Vargas to the Coup

During the Old Republic (from 1889 to 1930) the presidency, while nominally an elected post, was rotated by a series of preselection deals and electoral frauds, mainly involving the elites of Sao Paulo, Minas Gerais and Rio de Janeiro (the centre-south triangle in which much of the population and most of the industry were – and are – concentrated). In 1930, President Washington Luiz attempted to buck the established succession and instal his own nominee, Julio Prestes. A faction of mainly young, nationalist military officers intervened and ensured that the defeated candidate, Getulio Vargas, took up the presidency. So began the rule of one of the most skilful political jugglers in Brazilian history.

Vargas based his support on the nationalist elements within the bourgeoisie and the army, and on the growing numbers of urban industrial workers. The first groups benefited from the enormous industrial proliferation brought about by the great depression and the resulting collapse of Brazil's external trade. The working class was won over by the welfare and labour legislation Vargas introduced.

Vargas's balancing act in reconciling these often conflict-ing interests reflected a new political reality: henceforth, no one group would have total hegemony, as for example the sugar planters had enjoyed in earlier times. The relative decline of the power of rural interests and the takeover of the state bureaucracy by a rising white-collar professional group meant that direct state control was no longer in the hands of the owners of what had now become the economic mainstay – coffee.

While no leader could challenge the landowners with impunity, a populist rhetoric had become essential for political success. Nonetheless, the level of mass organisation remained low. Vargas, in his role as 'father of the poor', stressed the personal nature of his concessions to working-class aspirations: improvements in conditions were 'granted' by him rather than 'won' by any rank-and-file movement. In fact, following a

23

clumsy left-wing uprising in 1935 and growing agitation by the right-wing integralist group, Vargas moved to concentrate more power in his own hands. In 1937 he turned himself into a full-blown dictator by a coup d'etat which established the *Estado Novo* (New State) along European fascist lines.

During the second world war the process of nationalist industrial development continued, with Vargas extending state intervention in the economy and consolidating the 'gains' of the urban workers in a state-sponsored trade union system. Backed by the military and by those sections of the bourgeoisie which could see great advantages in Brazil breaking out of the narrow role of primary producer, the state during the Vargas years took on those long-term, very expensive and risky ventures which private entrepreneurs could not contemplate, such as building a national steel industry at Volta Redonda, near Rio. Meanwhile, tariffs and other assistance helped to make manufacturing industry profitable. Although discussion of the best development 'model' for Brazil was perennial, voices stressing the need for free trade and putting forward the theory of comparative advantage were muted. The fact that the United States and Western Europe were preoccupied fighting a war was an essential factor in generating the industrial growth of the period, although such good luck could not continue for ever, as we shall see later.

With the war drawing to a close, pressures for an end to Vargas's authoritarian rule mounted. Rallies, calls for an election, party manoeuvres and Vargas's own ambivalent attitude to the succession led the army to oust him in October 1945. It was notable that military force should be the final arbiter, as it had been in 1930. Styling itself 'guardian of the constitution', the army has intervened decisively at key moments in Brazilian history: this was not to be the last.

Enrico Dutra was sworn in as president in January 1946. The balance of political forces had changed considerably from the Vargas era, and the Dutra years saw a different economic philosophy applied.

To begin with, the party structure had become much more formalised. Toward the end of his rule, Vargas had set up two major new groups. The PTB (Brazilian Labour Party) garnered the votes of urban workers and some members of the left-wing

24

intelligentsia; the PSD (Social Democratic Party) embraced traditional rural influence-holders, some of the nationalist bourgeoisie and certain regional groups, particularly in Minas Gerais. In addition to these parties, there was the UDN (National Democratic Union), which took a much more 'liberal' view of economic policy, favouring foreign investment and being less willing to support domestic industries where foreign goods were cheaper. The Communist Party was also legal for two years from 1945 to 1947, the only time in Brazilian history that it has been able to operate above ground.

Thomas Skidmore has identified three competing philosophies of development emerging during the Dutra years (1946 to 1950):

(i) the neo-liberal, favouring balanced budgets, tight control of the money supply, free movement of capital and an open door to foreign investment;

(ii) the developmentalist-nationalist, having its origins in the *Estado Novo* and supported by the *tenentes* (young military officers of the sort who had brought Vargas to power in 1930) and the United Nations Economic Commission for Latin America. This view accepted the need for a combination of private capital and state intervention; and

(iii) the radical nationalist, stressing the inherently exploitative nature of the economic system and the inequality of international trade links. In this view, total transformation of the society was essential and imperialist sabotage an ever-present danger.[9]

Though none of these views was completely dominant, the first prevailed under Dutra's presidency. It sought to streamline Brazilian industry and concentrate on its most efficient sectors, but is chiefly remembered for the draining of the reserves of foreign currency built up under Vargas and for opening the door to an American takeover of some of the vital sectors of the economy. Although nationalist feeling was strong on some questions, so that, for example, Brazil's control of her energy sources was retained and Petrobras, the state oil monopoly, eventually came into being, even this was not achieved without intense debate and opposition from the proponents of the 'free market' approach. The post-war period saw increasing penetration by western interests, especially after US involvement in European reconstruction decreased from 1950 onwards.

With the cold war at its height, it is not surprising that this economic dimension was matched by a change in the terms of political discourse. Anti-communism became an important theme, with notions of hemisphere defence much in vogue. Later of course, the emphasis changed from paranoia against the enemy without to repression of internal 'subversion' – that is, the suppression of popular movements dissatisfied with the gross inequalities and injustices in Brazilian society.

During the Dutra years, Vargas had sat in the federal legislature as a PSD senator from his home state of Rio Grande do Sul. At the same time, he worked to establish his credentials as a reformed dictator become democratic elder statesman, ready to serve again. The PTB grew in numbers, and the philosophy of *trabalhismo*, which had always been one of Vargas's political strengths, drew together a sizeable movement. The combination of social welfare, anti-capitalist rhetoric and economic nationalism had strong appeal, strong enough to win Vargas the presidential election of October 1950.

His return to power in 1951 marked a stepping up of overt class hostility. In frequent speeches Vargas attacked the foreign companies which were taking over the country and repatriating huge profits at Brazilian expense. Such talk was very popular with the electorate, and Vargas was able to add to his support on the left by bringing Joao Goulart into his cabinet in 1953. Goulart, a young leftist with close links to the unions, later became president himself, and played a dramatic role in the lead-up to the 1964 military coup. However, such moves on Vargas's part were not calculated to win the support of the middle class or of the bourgeoisie, which was becoming increasingly international in its outlook through the extensive dependence on US investment and technology which went with the open door policy. At the same time, structural bottlenecks in the economy and inflation were undermining Vargas's position. A severe drought in the north-east compounded his government's problems. A build-up of military hostility to the nationalist-leftist line eventually made his continuation in power untenable, and in

26

1954, amid a storm of accusations, scandals and media attacks from the right, he committed suicide.

In the stunned aftermath of the Vargas regime, factions within the military disagreed over the extent to which they should continue to intervene in the civilian political process. A 'constitutionalist' view prevailed, and in 1956, the PSD candidate, Juscelino Kubitschek, was sworn in as president. His vice-president was Goulart, supported by the PTB.

Kubitschek's strategy was to carry on the Vargas line of reconciling, as far as possible, the interests of urban workers and the national bourgeoisie. To do this he went for accelerated economic growth, promising fifty years of progress in five. This was the period of the planning and development of the new national capital at Brasilia, and of a stepped-up inflow of foreign, mainly US investment ($743 million, compared with $350 million in the Vargas years). This money went mainly into high-profit consumer durables such as the newly developed motor vehicle industry. The concentration of foreign control in the most dynamic and capital-intensive sectors of the economy not only made economic independence for Brazil more unlikely than ever: it also underlined and aggravated the class contradictions between the national bourgeoisie – increasingly aligned with forces outside the country – and the poor, both urban and rural.

> In the competition to secure strategic positions in the economy, national private capital rapidly lost to foreign capital control of the movement towards industrialisation. Lastly, when the possibility of substituting home-produced goods for imports was exhausted, private Brazilian companies and groups had no other alternative than to submit to foreign interests.[10]

The consequences of such a policy are obvious: productivity increased but employment did not keep pace. Wages were forced down (by 1959, real industrial workers' wages in Guanabara were only 76 per cent of their 1940 level), the market shrank and the number of enterprises serving it declined, leaving fewer and larger firms. Because of monopoly or semi-monopoly conditions, companies were still able to raise prices, regardless of demand. In fact, prices rose *because* demand fell. By the early

27

sixties, inflation in Brazil was running at eighty to ninety per cent a year, and the domestic market was saturated.

In such conditions, the potential for class conflict was greatly enhanced. With the 'nationalist' section of the bourgeoisie weakened, and an increasing number of industrialists allied with foreign capital, whatever the cost to workers in terms of jobs or conditions, popular ferment was bound to grow, especially at a time when there was no direct military intervention in civil society. The late fifties and early sixties saw an upsurge of peasant movements, church and educational initiatives and demands for change from hitherto passive quarters. Agricultural workers' organisations were forming, particularly in the north-east, where Joao Firmino had founded the first Peasant League in 1956. The Catholic Church organised rural unions at the same time, partly to ameliorate the plight of the peasants and partly to ensure that some non-radical, non-leftist control over the people could be retained. Some of the leading churchmen were themselves very radical, and perhaps the most famous was the Archbishop of Recife, Dom Helder Camara. Wage and other demands were widespread as a result of all these groups' activities.

In politically aware circles, discussion centred around the issue of the fragile alliance between workers and bourgeoisie. Some still maintained that this was the correct path. Others, among them the Communist Party, denounced it as a dangerous illusion, seeing that the real interests of capital lay elsewhere. The true consciousness was class consciousness, they argued, not some woolly chauvinism which served only to cloud the basic question.

Kubitschek to Goulart: Popular Agitation and Counter-revolution

It should not be assumed that the state was totally oblivious of the problems faced by the poor, especially in the north-east. Kubitschek set up the *Instituto Superior de Estudos Brasileiros (ISEB)*, which served as an official/academic forum for discussions of Brazilian development, and in which Freire played a part. Kubitschek had also gone into government planning with the

28

Programma de Metas (Target Plan) for overall development of the country. And following the 1958 drought, funds for the north-east were channelled through the new Superintendency for the Development of the North-east (SUDENE) whose director was Celso Furtado, a noted economist and writer on Brazilian development, who was later to play an important part in national politics. Because it saw the need for structural change and agricultural reform, SUDENE was denounced as a hotbed of leftist agitation by the traditional elite.

In 1960, Janio Quadros succeeded Kubitschek. His seven-month spell in the presidency was marked by his attempts to circumvent traditional political processes and dispense with the compromises and deals previous presidents had seen as part of the job. In the face of threats from the military and a stone-walling congress, he resigned and handed over to his vice-president Goulart.

Goulart assumed a presidency with powers much curtailed, and saddled with a newly-created post of prime minister. He spent the next sixteen months making the business of govern-ment appear as difficult as possible, until a 1963 plebiscite abolished the post of prime minister and gave him back the former presidential powers. At the same time, he attempted to ride the swell of popular agitation by proposing agricultural reform and campaigning in rural areas. He encouraged the organisation of unions and formed the National Confederation of Agricultural Workers to unify the peasants. To some extent, this was an effort not to be outflanked on the left by Miguel Arraes, who had been elected governor of the state of Pernam-buco in 1962. Arraes adopted a style of government utterly different from that practised by old-guard politicians. He put teeth into minimum-wage laws, spent time in the villages and plantations discussing development with the peasants, and generally made them feel that they had a right to make demands for an improvement in their lot. The success of the Cuban revolution of 1959 meant that the US suddenly became more dependent upon Brazil for sugar, so that a rise in sugar prices made it easier to meet the workers' wage demands.

Clearly, the era of compromise was over. Reform and opposition to imperialism were essentially movements for the improvement of the state of the poor. Indeed, no peasant or workers' leader could win support without revolutionary slogans. By the same token, the middle class and bourgeoisie were greatly alarmed by Goulart and his populist stance. State governments, the military, the media and the public service were hostile. The left, however, was sure that an era of democratisation had arrived.

Then again, in the second half of 1963, Goulart's government found itself repeatedly deadlocked in battles with a congress unwilling to co-operate with democratic solutions to change, after the failure of the six months of reformist government of the 'positive left' [Santiago Dantas; Celso Furtado]. The last two years before the 1964 coup constituted the period which saw the most extensive development of radical and revolutionary groups and grouplets in Brazil.[11]

Goulart's shift away from the 'positive left' was one more step on the road to the coup. The PTB based Furtado-Dantas group had been entrusted with the management of the economy and the introduction of an economic stabilisation programme after Goulart regained full presidential power. They proposed a foreign borrowing scheme, a pruning of government expenditure and a three-year plan to attack structural bottlenecks, involving agricultural reform and the offering of technical and financial assistance to the peasants. The package was not the simplistic attack on working-class living standards that such plans usually represent: it involved basic reforms and the nationalisation of foreign power and communications firms. However, its main effect was to enrage both the far right and the far (or 'negative') left, whose chief spokesman was Leonel Brizola, Goulart's brother-in-law.

Goulart's response was to pigeon-hole the plan and move closer to Brizola. His attacks on right-wing groups alienated the petit bourgeoisie. The military began to plot, with groups of senior officers meeting to discuss the threat of subversion and the danger to discipline within the armed services themselves. Meanwhile, Goulart was calling for tax reform, nationalisation

30

of foreign-owned property, rent control, and other measures. He organised a series of mass rallies to mobilise support, which were followed by counter-demonstrations by the bourgeoisie. Marshall Castello Branco warned his fellow-officers to beware of Goulart's plans to use the unions to overthrow the constitution and turn the army into a 'people's army' on the communist model.

After the arrest of forty sailors engaged in efforts to unionise the navy, more than a thousand others mutinied. Goulart refused to allow the navy to punish them and the admiral in charge resigned. Goulart asked the unions for a list of nominations for a replacement. This was too much for the military to accept. Not only was the President inciting mob rule, he was undermining the established order of military discipline and violating the constitution. In April 1964, assuming its guardian-of-the-constitution post, the army and navy moved against Goulart and he fled into exile in Uruguay.

At first most civilian politicians expected that normal business would be resumed after a short interval. They engaged in their habitual infighting and jockeying for position in the new regime, not realising that the era of 'democratic' reforms had come to an end. Although the military was by no means united in its position, there was a strong feeling among many officers that traditional politics had been too corrupt and chaotic, a feeling which the post-coup squabbling among the civilians did nothing to assuage. Support for what the soldiers had done was strong in the middle class and bourgeoisie in the cities, as well as among the landowners. The guardians of the constitution moved rapidly to entrench their power. Existing political parties were abolished, and two new ones set up: ARENA (The Alliance for Democratic Renewal), and the MDB (Brazilian Democratic Movement) as a sort of 'opposition'. The president was no longer to be popularly elected – congress would elect him, and all congressional candidates were vetted by the military. By a series of Institutional Acts, the new rulers progressively took over more and more civil powers, trying political crimes in military courts, suppressing resistance, and building up surveillance organisations working to harass and murder leftists. It need hardly be said that Freire's literacy programme was one of the casualties of the purge. Economic and social policy were confided to a new group of technocrats, who designed and applied the 'model' which gave rise to the 'Brazilian miracle' on which so much has been written. In other words, social progress was halted in favour of high profits, and the distribution of wealth became more unequal than before. Brazil had been integrated into world capitalism on an altogether higher plane.

Two important lessons may be learned from the Brazilian case.

The first concerns the role of the national bourgeoisie. As has been suggested, debate about this was habitual, with most political leaders trying to balance the growing demands of urban workers against the need for profits to keep the system going. In retrospect though, it is clear that this policy had definite limits. With capital investment and movement increasingly internationalised, whatever 'national' bourgeoisie remained was likely to be small and marginal. The powerful would see nothing to gain in opposing foreign penetration. With hindsight, Miguel Arraes wrote:

> The popular movement could only rely on its own strength . . . the association of the influential sections of the Brazilian bourgeoisie with imperialism was not just an unfortunate and passing episode, a temporary halt in the national and democratic development of Brazilian capitalism. It was rather . . . a manifestation of the only type of capitalist development possible in Brazil. Yet this is development which is dependent and very one-sided, which dooms great masses of the population to under-employment and poverty, and which requires for its political system an authoritarian and oligarchic state in which the great power of the generals is complemented by the viciousness of its torturers.[12]

The second lesson has to do with the nature of political forces in a 'society in transition', as Freire calls Brazil. The characteristic style is a populist one, in which often 'enlightened' leaders try to mobilise and represent a poorly organised mass. Manipulation, demagoguery and melodrama mark such situations. Because the levels of mass organisation and class aware-

32

ness are low, the economic power is still in the hands of a ruling class whose interests are fundamentally anti-democratic. Populist leaders may indulge in horse-trading, high-wire balancing acts and other political tricks, but in the final analysis political power flows from control of the economic base. Nominal stewardship of formal political institutions is not enough. And under the structures created by Vargas, even trade unions were linked to the state, deriving their power from it. As Francisco Weffort, author of the introduction to the Portuguese edition of *Education: the Practice of Freedom* points out, ideologies are less important than personalities under these conditions.[13] The two parties Vargas founded were agents of patronage rather than centres of power.

Historically, says Weffort, a process of 'premature massification' has been taking place. Traditional rural loyalties have been dissolved, and the urban masses have been mobilised by the hardness of their lot. Nevertheless, they have yet to achieve a *class* awareness of their situation, despite having by now lost faith in the ability of the populist leadership to deliver the goods. If populism is defined as a phenomenon characterised by mass movements led by intellectuals who are often more 'aware' than their followers, then it is plain that the leaders, however well-intentioned, live by manipulation, rather than by simply expounding a well-articulated set of aims clearly understood by the mass. Ideally, the mass is well-organised and educated in class struggle. The weakness of the popular forces in Brazil, of course was that they were not so organised. There were many highly visible and articulate groups and individuals, but an apparatus linking workers throughout the country did not exist. Consequently, when the right wing struck, it met with virtually no opposition: 'This democratic game rapidly finished when it appeared to threaten the established structure. When the moment for revolution came, there was no-one there to fight.'[14]

Education and the Potential for Change

Naturally enough, most of the agitation for change went on outside of the formal political institutions. The system could not countenance or contain the kind of activism engaged in by

Freire, the peasant leagues, *Acao Popular* or any of the other groups working in the north-east at that time. Yet, of course, a formal education system does exist in Brazil. A brief look at some of its characteristic features may explain why Freire and the others tended not to use the traditional schools for their work.

From one point of view, the history of Brazilian education is a story of modest progress. Towards the end of the colonial period, eighty-five per cent of the free population, and virtually all the slaves, were illiterate. Even in 1940, more than half of the twenty-to-thirty age group could not read or write. By 1960 more than two-thirds of this group was literate, partly as a result of the expansion of primary education. In 1867 only about nine per cent of the seven-to-eleven age group attended school; a century later, the proportion was nearer two-thirds. At the secondary level, provision expanded enormously to meet rising middle-class demand after the second world war: enrolment went up by 251 per cent between 1950 and 1964, while the population increased by only fifty-four per cent.

But figures can be used to support almost any point of view. The fallacy behind the steady-expansion theory is that it could be pursued to total literacy and total equality, or at least 'equality of opportunity, under the existing social structure. Our analysis of the nature of Brazilian development suggests otherwise. Firstly, there are important regional imbalances. The education budget for Sao Paulo during the sixties was two and a half times the national per capita average; for the north-east, it was one-fifth on the average. Secondly, there are urban/rural differences: in 1964, eighty-three per cent of the seven-to-eleven group in the towns and cities of Brazil as a whole were in school. In the towns and cities of the north-east the figure was at most seventy-eight per cent, and in the rural north-east fifty-three per cent.

Thirdly, the nature of participation is much less favourable than the simple figures on growth imply. Wastage and repeat rates have always been high, especially in primary school, and naturally those most at risk are the poor. For example, of those in the first year of primary school in 1945, only four per cent completed the fourth year in minimum time. Even as late as 1962,

34

only just over half of those completing fourth year went up to the *ginasio* (middle school), and only about half of them finished the *ginasio*. Repeats cause a bunching of older children in the primary school; so in the first grade in 1962, for every hundred children of the right age (six to eleven), there were 355 older ones. In the north, north-east and central-west the ratio was higher. In fact, in that year more than half of all primary pupils were in the first grade. Experience in virtually all underdeveloped countries has shown that poor parents struggle to send one child to school for one year. If the child is forced to repeat, or has to miss school to help with the harvest, to look after other children, or for any other reason, the chances of completion drop steeply after the first year. Where more than one child is involved, the problem is obviously compounded. In other words, a powerful *economic* selection is operating to preserve the status quo.

All this is very clear. What is not so self-evident to many proponents of this sort of educational pyramid is the way in which apparently progressive policies serve to promote inequality, often despite the good intentions of the planners. Any sensible person would support the extension of basic primary education to all children, both as a measure of social justice and as a way of producing a more creative and civic-minded workforce. Then, it must be accepted that in a poor country with limited resources secondary education is more of a luxury and can only be offered to the most talented, who will provide the nation's high-level labour power. Finally, higher education is even more costly than secondary, and therefore some government subsidy for students is required. The effect of these three 'sensible' policies is that although most children get some experience of school, entry to secondary school is heavily biased in favour of children from better-off homes. Consequently, in addition to the selection which takes place in primary school, the lack of universal secondary education raises another barrier to social mobility for the lower orders. Further, the group entering higher education is bound to be largely made up of middle- and upper-class children. To subsidise education at this level out of federal government funds, as Brazil does, is therefore to transfer resources from the poor to those who need subsidies least. Looked at in this way, the structure of education, at first sight

35

designed in keeping with the needs of the nation, becomes a highly regressive instrument of class discrimination.

These contradictions appear even more marked if we examine the nature of the schooling process in Brazil. Foreign influences, for example, have played an important role in educational development. First there were the Jesuits, who started schools for the children of the aristocracy in the mid-sixteenth century. In 1759 they were expelled because their anti-absolutist views, desire for freedom from secular control, and loyalty to Rome conflicted with the commonly-held enlightenment position. European ideas continued to be imported at other phases of the country's history: for example, during the Napoleonic period there was a vogue for more technically-oriented schools along the lines of the French *lycées*. Of course the numbers attending these schools were never very great, because the economic base, with its primary-product structure and low level of capitalisation did not require many technically-educated people.

The post-independence development of liberal industrialism brought a demand for the achievement of universal primary education as a means to universal suffrage. In addition, the free enterprise ideology of individual self improvement was not at odds with a 'meritocratic' secondary system, so that the most able could rise to the top and benefit the 'nation' by their individual efforts. This philosophy of enlightened self interest evolved logically in the twentieth century to come under the influence of Deweyan progressivism. Again, the liberal approach stressed individual development and the role of the school as an agency to socialise children to 'fit in' comfortably with society. Unfortunately, when the society is hierarchical and oppressive, this has unpleasant implications, which we must now develop.

As well as being harshly selective, Brazilian education has always discriminated in the *kind* of schooling received by those lucky enough to get in. Children of less well-off families were likely, if they completed primary school, to go on to some sort of vocational or technical education. The better-off took an academic secondary education which was severely formal, dominated by rote-learning of theoretical knowledge, and did not prepare them for a particular career:

36

The brilliant theoretical arguments developed in Brazil in favour of humanistic, and against practical, education; in support of intellectual, and in opposition to vocational utilitarian training, were mere rationalisations. They enveloped with rhetoric the conservative goals of a society subtly divided into a leisure elite and the masses.[15]

When children are taught that school is a means of self-advancement, and that life-chances are dependent on length of schooling, they naturally seek to stay in school as long as possible and to use this ladder to escape and rise out of their present positions. Hence the phenomenon of urban drift, observed in all countries where school has this function. All underdeveloped countries face the problem of primary school leavers, as well as secondary graduates, flocking to the cities in search of jobs which do not exist in anything like the numbers required. When these people do not get the jobs they want, they live by crime, petty services, staying with relatives and friends and getting by on their wits. And for societies which desperately need to use their most educated and physically most productive members to the full, they are a major waste of resources. Yet they are doing no more than the system has taught them to do. Thus we have the idiot spectacle, commonly observed in third world countries, of a political leader lecturing young students about the need to go back to the villages and work for national development. The leader then climbs into a Mercedes and returns to government house. Predictably, the students are less swayed by the leader's words than by his actions.

The corollary of all this is that the *content* of education becomes largely irrelevant, in the sense that things are not learned in school to be applied in life. What counts is the type of school attended and the piece of paper obtained at the end. The selection function of schooling, in other words, is more important than its part in maximising productive forces. As a result, the traditional academic education which the Brazilian elite has always received is the most desirable for every student, since every student has been taught to desire elite membership. The expansion of secondary education in post-war Brazil was the outcome of just this sort of petit-bourgeois pressure to join the upper classes. And since the result obtained at the top of the school system sets the pattern right back through the schools, the formal academic curriculum is the norm even where it would seem least appropriate.

> The rural school curriculum continues to be dominated by the value-orientations and self-perpetrating interests of the urban middle strata and elites who emphasise the non-instrumental and status-conferring functions of formal education.[16]

Not only is the formal curriculum divisive and dysfunctional: by stressing a consensual view of society and teaching respect for tradition and the established order, the very ethos of the schools turns into a barrier to genuine development:

> The tendency is for the model rural school in Latin America to develop competitive and authoritarian relationships, while alienating students from their environments.[17]

In the light of all this, it is not surprising that Freire chose to set up cultural circles outside of the formal system. If the aim of education is to produce people who are able to develop some autonomy, and the ability to think critically and act collectively to change the world, the school system is highly unsuitable. Freire's view of social relations in Brazil, like that of the Catholic radicals in the MEB (Basic Education Movement) was influenced by existentialism, and by the notion of a patron-dependent dichotomy. Especially in rural areas, the most significant relationship is between oligarch and impoverished, *polo dominante* and *polo dominado* – the two opposing poles of the social spectrum, with very little in between them. Official education, however well-intentioned, has as its goal an acceptance of what is, rather than a mobilisation towards what ought to be, that is domestication rather than liberation. To move from one to the other 'would thus require an active, dialogical educational programme concerned with social and political responsibility, and prepared to avoid the danger of massification'.[18]

3. The Politics of Literacy
by Barbara Bee

Literacy is a two-edged sword.
It can be repressive or liberating.[1]

Paulo Freire's principal concern during his time in Brazil was for the vast numbers of illiterate people, estimated at sixteen million aged fourteen years and over. He sought to popularise and make available to them an education which need not take place in a traditional school. Together with his colleagues, Freire launched 'culture circles' in the villages and slum areas of Recife as an alternative. They were deliberately designed to be as unlike school programmes as possible: in place of a teacher, there would be a co-ordinator; instead of the traditional lecture and handing down of information, an exchange of ideas between people in the form of 'dialogue'; instead of passive pupils, there would be active group participants; instead of material which was far removed from the interests and understanding of the participants, there would be compact programmes broken down into manageable and meaningful learning units. The purpose of these culture circles was to attempt, through group debate, 'either to clarify situations or to seek action arising from that clarification'.[2]

Topics for debates in the culture circles included nationalism, profit remittances abroad, the political evolution of Brazil, development, illiteracy, the vote for illiterates, and democracy. These topics were introduced with slides or pictures and followed by discussion. Generally encouraged by the results of this form of participatory teaching and the level of discussion and dialogue which resulted, Freire became even more convinced that learning to read should be, for adults, a process in which the actual content and material had bearing on their daily reality. Moreover, a study of the problems should lead to critical awareness of

39

the possibilities for action and change. Thus the chief object of the literacy process was not one of mere technical mastery of the written word, but a quality of consciousness, a changed awareness which the people could express through language and action. As Freire put it: 'I treated literacy as more than a mechanical problem, and linked it to *conscientiazacao*, which was dangerous'.[3]

The task of motivating the Brazilian people was a difficult one. They were apathetic, downtrodden, and fatalistic in their attitudes. In order to change this demoralising situation into something more positive and responsive Freire and his team needed to convince the people of their own worth, to show them that no matter how denuded of dignity they considered themselves to be, they were in fact makers of culture, of history, and subjects in life, not merely objects of manipulation. A literacy programme was thus developed based on an anthropological concept of culture and the difference between 'nature', which humans did not make, and 'culture', which they create and re-create. Freire believed that in discussing this distinction illiterates would be enabled to see that they contribute as much to history and culture as literate people. The people would become aware that they can know as conscious beings, and therefore can act upon their world to transform it. Significant in that distinction was the power of language – both oral and written – in enabling illiterates to emerge, through discussion and critical reflection, from ignorance and opinion to knowledge and understanding. So what the illiterate would gain from an examination of the anthropological concept of culture would be an awareness of:

> the distinction between the world of nature and the world of culture; the active role of people in and *with* their reality; the role of mediation which nature plays in relationships and communication among the people; culture as an addition made by people to a world they did not make; culture as the result of the labour of men and women; of their efforts to create and re-create; the transcendental meaning of human relationships; the humanistic dimension of culture; but as creative assimilation, not as

40

information storing: the democratisation of culture; the learning of reading and writing, as a key to the world of written communication. In short, the role of men and women as subjects in the world, and with the world.[4]

By this approach to education and literacy Freire and his colleagues hoped the masses would gradually lose their fatalistic, apathetic and naive view of the world and the word as unalterably given, replacing it with critical awareness and acceptance of their role as subjects in and of the world, whose presence and existence demanded action as well as critical thought.

Francisco Brenand, one of the greatest contemporary Brazilian artists, was asked to draw a series of 'codified pictures' that would generally introduce the concept of culture to the people.[5] Each picture was to be used to stimulate discussion and awareness about a different aspect of culture, and its role in the lives of people. The pictures were deliberately kept bold and simple and were styled in such a way that illiterates could recognise and readily identify with them. The sequence of ten was carefully arranged so as to draw out the connection between the culture-making capacities of people and their communicative capacities. Using a slide projector and blank walls of houses in the villages, slides were presented in turn. When slide number one was shown the co-ordinator asked the illiterates to name all the objects they could see in the picture. This was because they were not used to graphic representation, and might not identify what was meant to be shown. Then, the co-ordinator led the discussion into the distinction between nature and culture by asking a variety of questions about the pictures. Who made the well? Why? What materials were used? Who made the tree? How is it different from the well? Who made the pigs, the birds, the man? Who made the house, the hoe, the book? In this way the group gradually discovered that people use natural materials to change their situation, to create culture. Non-literates might be aware of this distinction but the discussion enabled them to name and clarify their knowledge. This process emphasised that they too were makers of culture, and therefore cultured.

Once the group had recognised and understood the

41

distinction between the worlds of nature and culture, and people's role in each, the co-ordinator presented situations which focused on and expanded other aspects of culture. The groups discussed culture as a systematic acquisition of human experience, and discovered that in a lettered culture this acquisition isn't confined to oral transmission, as with unlettered cultures, which lack graphic signs. The last slide enabled the group to develop critical consciousness – to look at itself and reflect on its own activity. The picture showed a circle of culture in progress, so participants could easily identify it as representing themselves. The co-ordinator introduced the phrase 'democratisation of culture' to be discussed in the light of what had been happening in the meetings. The function of culture was critically examined by everyone – what they had gained from the experience, what dialogue was, and what it meant to enrich one's consciousness. Freire speaks of the increase in self-awareness and self-confidence that came to the participants in the course of the meetings, of their enthusiasm and emergent understanding of their significance in the world.

> All these discussions are critical, stimulating, and highly motivating. The illiterate perceives critically that it is necessary to learn to read and write, and prepares him- or herself to become the agent for this learning.[6]

The concept of 'conscientisation' is fundamental to Freire's understanding of literacy and education. He maintains that the educative process is never neutral and that persons are either educated for domestication or liberation. Where there exists a dominant culture of silence, people are taught to accept what is handed down to them by the ruling elite. They live only to carry out unthinkingly and unquestioningly orders from above. Their understanding of reality is limited to what they are told to accept and believe – the myths that keep them silent and in ignorance. However, when education and literacy liberate they shatter the silence and bring people to an awareness of their condition and to their democratic rights to participate in making decisions regarding the problems of their existence. Freire writes:

> acquiring literacy does not involve memorising sentences,

words and syllables – lifeless objects unconnected to an existential universe – but rather an attitude of creation and re-creation, a self transformation producing a stance of intervention in one's context.[7]

It isn't sufficient, argues Freire, for illiterates to psychologically and mechanically dominate reading and writing techniques. They must dominate these techniques in terms of consciousness, to understand what is read, what is written and why one writes. This cannot possibly be achieved if the educator, or teacher, remains aloof from his or her pupils and merely donates skills and information as one who knows. The role of the educator is to enter into dialogue with illiterates about concrete situations and offer them the instruments with which they can teach themselves to read and write. Such teaching cannot be imposed from the top, as it were, but can only take place in a shared investigation, in a problem-raising situation between educator and educatee. Thus the learning of content and the learning process are inextricably bound together.

Because dialogue characterises the relationship between the illiterate and the teacher, there can be no reliance on set, commercial texts which, Freire claims, set up certain groupings of graphic signs as a gift, and cast the illiterate in the role of the object rather than the subject of his learning. Primers, or reading books, donate or give to the illiterate words and sentences which should preferably arise from his own creative effort.

A parallel situation in the English-based school system would be one where we introduce young children to reading schemes and packaged library kits, without listening to or dwelling upon the children's own language, thoughts, feelings and experiences. In such a situation the teacher can do no more than teach words and meanings, which may well be alien to the child's understanding. If, however, teachers are using the children's own experiences as the basis for reading and writing, then there has to be discussion and clarification between teacher and pupils if genuine creative communication is to take place and this will result in the children wishing to read and write down their experiences in due course.

Acting on the assumption that adults, and children too, can

learn to read with easy words that are familiar and meaningful to them Freire and his literacy teams developed what he calls 'generative words', rather than primers, meaning those words whose syllabic elements offered, through recombination, the creation of new words. Before a reading programme was introduced in any specific community, Freire's teams invited that community, with help from volunteers, to investigate its culture. Together they examined all the familiar activities and habits of the community and made note of significant words used by them. From there they developed a short list of words based on two criteria – the word's emotional impact and significance for provoking discussion, and its phonetic value in presenting all the sounds of Portuguese. They discovered that no more than eighteen words were necessary for teaching adults to read and write syllabic, phonetic languages such as Portuguese and Spanish. These words were 'generative' in the sense that they could generate among illiterates critical discussion of the social and political realities of their lives, what Freire called 'problematising their existential situations'. By breaking the eighteen words into syllables and rearranging them, non-literates could generate and transcribe other words. The sequence in which the words were presented was carefully prepared. The initial word was tri-syllabic and each of the three syllables consisted of one consonant and one vowel. Second, less common and more difficult phonetic material was placed at the end of the list. Third, words that named concrete and familiar objects were to appear early, whilst words dealing with more abstract, social and political realities were to appear later. Thus, a list which was prepared for use in the state of Rio, a rural area and satellite of the city of Rio de Janeiro, began with 'fa-ve-la' meaning a slum, and ended with 're-qu-ez' meaning riches and wealth.

Freire wanted the ideas represented by the words to be critically discussed before the words themselves were analysed as graphic symbols. So the teams prepared pictures to illustrate each word. For example, in order to illustrate the word brick – 'tijolo' – a picture of a building construction scene was used. This was presented at first without the word 'tijolo' added. Then in the third picture or slide, the word 'tijolo' appeared above. On all the lists the first word invariably has three syllables. The reason for

44

this was that a chart could be made of the syllables of tri-syllabic words in a way which helped non-literates to understand the structure of Portuguese words. Thus, the co-ordinator after introducing '*tijolo*' broke the word into syllables. The group read aloud the individual syllables, then the co-ordinator presented the first one, – '*ti*' – like this: '*ta*', '*te*', '*ti*', '*to*', '*tu*'. At first only '*ti*' was recognised but by reading aloud the five syllables, the groups learned that the '*t*' sound was constant and they learned the sound of the five vowels. Next '*jo*' was presented in the same manner, followed by '*lo*'. Finally all three were combined in a chart called the 'card of discovery' as shown here:

ta	*te*	*ti*	*to*	*tu*
ja	*je*	*ji*	*jo*	*ju*
la	*le*	*li*	*lo*	*lu*

After one horizontal and one vertical reading the group was asked to put together other words by combining the syllables on the card of discovery in different ways e.g. '*lutu*' – struggle, '*loja*' – store, '*lote*' – lot. So long as the group was busy discovering the mechanism for combining syllables, co-ordinators were trained not to be concerned about accepting combinations which did not make words, so long as the principle was being understood. In summary, then, the life *and* vocabulary of the community were investigated.

Co-ordinators were carefully chosen with a view to using only those who could empathise and dialogue with the people. A circle of culture of 25-30 non-literates was organised to meet every week night for one hour during six to eight weeks. The early sessions were devoted to analysing the ten pictures illustrating the distinctions between nature and culture. At about the ninth session the first generative word was introduced. At the end of the session participants were asked to make up words from the card of discovery and to bring their lists to the next meeting. At the remaining sessions the other seventeen or so generative words were introduced one by one. Participants practised writing and reading aloud, they expressed opinions and wrote them down, they examined newspapers and discussed local issues. Those who completed the literacy course could read and write simple tasks, make something of the local newspapers and discuss Brazilian problems. The whole process took between 30-40 hours to complete.

Freire and his colleagues were planning a post-literacy curriculum based on the investigation of Brazilian themes carried out in the circles of culture. Their expectation was for 20,000 literacy circles to be operating in Brazil in 1964 but the military coup stopped the programme, a sign that his literacy campaign for liberation of the people was more than a little threatening to the imposed culture of silence. Regarding this Freire has written,

> Because of this I was jailed. Of course if I had developed only a formal way of teaching I would still be in my country. But to the extent that I challenged people to unveil the elites of power, they could not accept me and they were absolutely right from their point of view. They would have been naive not to have put me in jail. I had to be punished by them. I understand this well, as I will punish them when I can.[8]

The people who see Freire as having only to do with techniques of literacy, while choosing to ignore the political implications of conscientisation, miss the point of his teaching. Freire certainly wanted to teach adult illiterates the mechanical skills of reading and writing, but he did so with the deliberate aim and intention of awakening them to, and liberating them from, their naive acceptance of life and its dehumanising effects upon them. The political nature of his work is prominent and undeniable:

> I have only one desire: that my thinking may coincide historically with the unrest of all those who, whether they live in those cultures which are wholly silenced or in the silent sectors of cultures which prescribe their voice, are struggling to have a voice of their own.[9]

Yet it is a mistake to locate him in the context only of third world countries. We in the first world have long taught children and adults to read and write under the guise of neutrality, considering the literacy process to be more a matter of technical know-how than values and attitudes. We can learn much from Freire's contention that when we enable people to read and write, we can also present them either with a world view that is clouded and mystifying, or enable them to clarify and understand their life situation more clearly. This is achieved not only by what we teach, but why and how. What do we mean when we say a person develops from being a non-reader, or that an 'illiterate' has become a reader and literate? What distinctions are there to be made between a person who is 'functionally literate' and a person who is 'fully literate', if we may coin such a phrase? Once we begin to examine the basic assumptions behind these descriptions it becomes obvious that there is an ideology and practice which is undeniably political in effect, even when we try actively to make the process of acquiring literacy nothing more than the mastery of a technical skill. The written word can subdue, deceive, pacify, and lull, or it can arouse, enlighten, stimulate and awaken depending on the ideology and practice employed. In short, education can be for domestication or liberation.

Commonly the term 'functionally literate' is used to refer to those whose literacy skills are adequate for carrying out those actions required of them by their society. The aims of a programme based on the acquisition of functional literacy may be summarised in one sentence: 'to make people become more efficient and productive citizens and workers under the prevailing governments'.[10] Functional literacy programmes enable people to apply for jobs, fill in their income tax form, understand documents from authorities and generally practise the language skills verbally and in written form. But the purpose behind such programmes is an economic one:

> Throughout a diversity of situations the aim of functional literacy remains basically the same; to mobilise, train and educate still insufficiently utilised labourpower to make it more productive.[11]

Programmes in functional literacy, undertaken by organisations such as UNESCO are both specific, in that they are confined to those countries and areas where there is evidence of progress and modernisation and where goals of economic development are apparent, and also intensive, in that they concentrate on persons having some definable skill which can be tapped and utilised in

47

the interests of the economy. As a consequence functional literacy programmes may be defined as:

> *intensive* rather than extensive, *selective* rather than *widespread*, geared to *employment* rather than culture, and as a first step towards producing qualified working power.[12] [emphasis in original]

So, when one compares functional literacy programmes with the kind of programme Freire advocates we find that there are marked differences in intent and purpose. Functional literacy is more a donation to the people, a creation by experts which is handed down to selected groups to serve a definite purpose. The educational contents and methods are adapted to keep the participants at a level which the donors consider desirable. Its originators are often closely allied to private business enterprises which have financial interests in developing countries.

Freire's work in Guinea-Bissau is an excellent example of a literacy programme which has every intention of avoiding the pitfalls of functional literacy in the name of technological progress. There, on the invitation of the government of this recently independent African country, Freire is pioneering methods of involving the peasants in the mastery of words and numbers so the whole populace, and not merely a few self-selected leaders, are being taught to read and compute in a meaningful and critical way. Freire is convinced that literacy work has more relevance when related to the introduction of new production techniques and the need to increase the community's ability to take charge of its own development by providing its own basic services. The emphasis in Guinea-Bissau is on educating adults, who can, in turn, pass on to the children what they learn. As in Recife, Freire's basic approach is via social issues – housing, work, health and food. His aim, 'to concretise many of their dreams, by working against injustice in a very open way',[13] has not altered either.

All too often literacy education is seen as a means to economic and technological expansion. Freire, while not denying the need for development, is severely critical of mechanistic approaches to both literacy and education, arguing that mass production as an organisation of human labour is one of the most potent instruments of exploitation.

> By requiring people to behave mechanically, mass production domesticates them. By separating their activity from the total project, requiring no total critical attitude towards production, it dehumanises them. By excessively naming a person's specialisation, it constructs his or her horizons, making of him or her a passive fearful naive being. And therein lies the chief contradiction of mass production: whilst amplifying people's sphere of participation it simultaneously distorts this amplification by reducing their critical capacity through exaggerated specialisation.[14]

The only certain way to avoid the danger of massification, according to Freire, is not to reject technology but to make people critically conscious and able to resist its potentially dehumanising and silencing effects upon their lives. Functional literacy does little to touch the consciousness of the illiterate in a way which Freire argues it should. It offers the recipients no opportunities to make decisions, but encourages passivity and acceptance and, ultimately, a retreat from democracy. The only valid form of literacy training is one which enables the learner to intervene in reality, to experience responsibility at all levels: in schools, trade unions, places of employment, neighbourhoods, churches and rural communities. Literacy must serve the purpose of teaching people how to demythologise and decode their culture. Functional literacy, allied to a lack of critical consciousness, simply leads to the further oppression of men and women. Moreover, it creates the culture of silence in which the masses are mute. They may be able to read and write, but they are alienated from the power responsible for their silence. Thus the functionally literate never learn that their action upon the world is transforming, that they might voice their thoughts, feelings and attitudes about the kind of society they see as desirable. Functional literacy does just what its title suggests. It enables one to function, rather than dynamically interact with and transform one's society.

If a person is to become genuinely literate as opposed to functionally literate, a quality of critical reflection must be

49

engendered in the pedagogical methods. Without reflection and analysis of the cultural milieu, literacy becomes something handed out and isolated from life's realities. Hence Freire's emphasis on context and coherence is crucial. Being able to read is itself no guarantee of being either civilised or uncivilised, moral or immoral. As Wayne O'Neil points out in his essay 'Properly literate', 'One can hate or kill with it or without it. In fact a nation can kill better with it – no argument for phonics or look and say.'[15]

Technically speaking, being able to read means the ability to follow words across a page and understanding generally what is superficially there. The sad fact about schools is that they so often succeed in teaching children to read, but in the process they destroy literacy. Schools do not consider the context of the learner significant unless it coincides with the social values and ideology of the school. All too often the methods and materials employed are pre-packaged ahead of the child's actual experience. Reading is taught as if language was a mystery beyond the reach of all but the smart few. So the young child who comes to school bubbling with life, and the ability to make some meaning of the experiences that characterise her or his existence, is taught to sit down, be quiet, and listen to a highly abstract representation of sounds and symbols which seem, and often are, a million miles away from the language that the child already has, and the largely intuitive grasp on reality it possesses. The inexorable process of making the child the object, rather than the subject, of his or her learning has begun. Reading seems to be another world. Children may learn the sheer mechanisms of the process, but in so doing, they lose something of themselves and the understanding that the written and spoken word have relevance for them. They learn to read superficially, to skate over areas of knowledge that are compartmentalised and reduced to descriptive jargon. Little or nothing that underlies the child's awareness, uttering or comprehension is allowed to penetrate this veil of neutrality that hides the real world of meaning from the children's eyes. So they emerge from fifteen years schooling being able to read, but far from literate. To quote Wayne O'Neil again: 'Learning to read is no huge obstacle to leap. Schools simply guard the chambers of the elite, throw up the barri-

50

cades.'[16] He shows that trying to make reading fit into a pre-ordained context is the first, most destructive phase of denying coherence. He pleads for recognition and acceptance of the child's own language and context:

> Let them learn to read. Don't teach them. Let it emerge as they go about talking and telling of the riches they already possess. Forget word frequency counts. Who could work up any interest in the hundred most frequent words in any language? Keep all the words and the world together and them involved in it.[17]

This is powerful advocacy for Freire's approach to literacy and one which it is possible to promote in all educational contexts – be they kindergartens, secondary schools, or adult institutions. The important thing to note is the plea for the recognition of the children's voices and the validity of their culture, particularly where it differs from mainstream or middle-class culture.

A successful example of this is the work of Sylvia Ashton-Warner, a primary school teacher, whose activities in the field of literacy are recorded in her book *Teacher*.[18] Sylvia Ashton-Warner's ethnic primers grew out of experiences with Maori children amongst whom she worked in New Zealand. When she first arrived at the school all she could find in the way of books to teach reading were those based on white, protestant culture. These were alien and oppressive to Maori children whose lives were being lived out in a community where birth, celebration, copulation and death were as much a part of their experience as the spirit world their elders believed in. So Ashton-Warner listened to the children talking among themselves, and with her, and found the words that had significance for them – such as Mummy, Daddy, ghost, live, hit, baby, fight. These became the basis of the children's language programme and reading material so that they learned quickly and easily without the merest hint that reading might be mystifying and hard.

We can see in the work of Ken Worpole from a school in Hackney, London, a similar approach. His fourth form boys produced storybooks for younger boys in the school, and were encouraged to articulate their own particular sense of themselves

51

and their situation, over and against definitions imposed on them from the outside. The boys concerned not only wrote the books based on the characters of two younger boys in the school, but they provided the illustrations as well, using photographs of the local area where the boys played, thus giving the story authenticity. The language and syntax in the books were precisely those used by the children themselves – their 'generative' words, rather than those of a teacher. Worpole notes that not only was the whole venture an important educational and social experience, but that the group learned new ways of working together. The concept of authority as something remote and alien began to lose its traditional aura. The activity of writing acquired a genuine social purpose where pupils helped each other. Worpole's whole approach to the question of literacy is to ground his teaching in the possibilities that the new media technology makes available, with a view to democratising the cultural process. He writes:

> At present our system of education is based on the idea of the children as passive consumers of knowledge which perhaps prepares them too neatly for their adult functions as consumers of material and cultural production. We perform disservice to the children we teach if we confirm them in their roles as consumers only, or, by practice, never suggest that their writing is anything more than 'self-expression'. In short, they must become authors and we have to locate their audience, and to make available to them the means of production.[19]

The US writer Herbert Kohl points out ways in which educators and teachers can challenge the culture of silence. People can be made critically conscious of how language is used to confound and mystify, and come to see that concepts like 'justice' and 'equality' are relative. Thus, black children reading history books written with the white, oppressive culture in mind have to re-evaluate words like 'progress' and 'discovery' and learn that the language of history is value-laden, self-justifying and subjective, never value-free, objective or neutral. Kohl agrees with Worpole in seeing that every community ought to devise its own programme for the teaching of reading and writing, by reference to an understanding of its people, customs,

52

dialect (if any), significant features and relationships. Taught in this way reading would begin with the people, it would be by and for them. Words in isolation would be abandoned. Those which have meaning and relevance, and which emerge from talking and discussing particular social situations and political contexts, would be all-important. This, in due course, would become the basis for reading thoughts and feelings, as Kohl observes:

> the real pin-pointing and thinking about language – one's own language and other people's language – seems to come both in the act of writing and in the creation of stories, in the making of language of one's own and then recording it and sharing it with other people.[20]

Just as Freire's methods give back to the people a sense of self and their own worth, so the process of reading and writing in our schools must enhance a sense of personal and cultural identity. This has not been the case with the poor and oppressed in our societies. The myth of cultural deprivation is a powerful one which often leads minority cultures and the poor to accept labels of 'deprived' and 'disadvantaged'. It is especially apparent in areas of language and reading, where deficiencies and prejudices in the education system tend rather to be blamed on the background of the children. Differences in cultural life-styles have been looked upon as 'deficiencies', and compensatory programmes such as Project Headstart in the United States have been donated to the poor and cultural minorities ostensibly to bring them up to standard. The standard implied is, of course, middle class and competitive. In reality, one culture is research-ing another without really understanding it, and the so-called 'deprived' are compared not with middle-class reality but with middle-class ideals. Thus what are merely differences in history, culture, life-style, and ways of using language come to be seen as inferior. Teachers discriminate against certain children and oppress them because those children bring to the classroom different ways of speaking and acting from those traditionally assumed to be most useful in climbing the meritocratic ladder.

Teachers of literacy have to do with their particular content and context what Freire did with the programmes he used with the Brazilian people: instil motivation and change the content of what is presented if it invalidates, denudes or denigrates the worth of the learner. If teachers can impart to children, particularly those from minority cultures, a strong sense of their own worth and creative input in the world, then we are also giving to them an increasing power to transform oppressive conditions. For too long schools, by their emphasis on reading and language schemes, have ignored, rejected or deliberately set out to silence those who would speak with a different voice and accent from the dominant and accepted middle-class voice and expression. Somewhere between our lofty conception of what constitutes 'high culture' and what we like to refer to condescendingly as 'mass culture', we have silenced the voices of vast numbers of children and adults. Sylvia Ashton-Warner turned her back on primers that she believed offended the dignity of her Maori pupils and instead encouraged them to talk and discourse on what had meaning, fear, joy, delight, pain and pleasure in their lives. She not only released a stream of words and images that are striking in their richness and warmth, but more importantly she gave expression to the children's humanity.

Freire reminds us that the interests of oppressors lie in changing the consciousness of the oppressed not the situation which oppresses them; for the more the oppressed can be led to adapt to that situation, the more easily they can be dominated. So teachers beware! Much of the literature on cultural deprivation rests on the assumption that so-called 'deprived' and 'disadvantaged' children must be helped, via special language and reading schemes to catch up with their more fortunate middle-class counterparts. Never a suggestion that perhaps there might be something wrong with the school or society. Harold Rosen makes it clear that we must choose between perpetuating the culture of silence or breaking it. Not to choose is to side with the oppressor: it is not neutrality.

It is becoming increasingly difficult to refuse to take sides. We have to choose between descriptions of an impoverished restricted code and the unearthing of a living oral tradition, between visions of school as a civilised and well-ordered island in a sea of barbarism and anomie and the aspiration that they should be re-incarnated through the

> nourishment of the neighbourhood and community, be-
> tween reading 'schemes' and literacy through critical
> consciousness. Indeed all the choices we make, minute,
> urgent, even trivial, are more and more seen as taking sides.
> English teaching has become overtly a political matter.[21]

Rosen's essay is a persuasive plea for teachers to see their children not as emanating from desirable or undesirable homes, high or low cultures, but as socially constituted human beings who can draw sustenance for the imagination from their own world and its values. Deeply critical of a literacy approach that is designed merely to foster personal sensitivity, personal response and self-exploration, Rosen argues these are inadequate for the child who faces the prospect of a job which cannot do other than destroy its spirit. Reading and writing may seem almost intrinsically irrelevant for many working-class children because they are not linked with the social context of the child's experience. The result is a 'culture-clash'. What literacy teaching must do is veer away from the notion of a verbally individualistic reflective activity, and come instead to see literacy as a form of cultural production.

Freire's concept of literacy entails a quality of consciousness. It is not simply the gaining of technical skills which enable us to read and write. Literacy encourages the oppressed to speak and value language, as a tool for perceiving that society is not fixed and unchangeable; but that its structures and institutions can be challenged and transformed through concerted thought and action. Illiterates thus become not mere 'objects' submerged in a silent reality, but 'subjects' in and with the world. The real worth of Freire's literacy method is not that he enabled adults to read and write in forty hours, but that he gave them the power to think for themselves. He showed them how they could be the architects of their own collective liberation. In many first world schools, literacy functions as a form of social control by which some are enabled to benefit while others are held back on grounds of disadvantage, whether economic or social. Literature and literacy schemes are saturated with political bias – sometimes overt, sometimes implied, in the forms of sexism, racism, and class prejudice. Yet teachers go on claiming neutrality and impartiality in the mistaken belief that by so doing they are enabling children to make up their own minds. In effect they are helping to perpetuate the very myths which prevent equality in society and which keep people in their so-called place. We do well to remember that literacy is a two-edged sword. It is a weapon for maintaining or transforming the received order of social relations.

4. Education for Awareness: A talk with Paulo Freire*
by Rex Davis

Risk:

I have seen your new book, Pedagogy of the Oppressed. *In it the idea that education is either for the domestication of people or the liberation of people is a very clear theme. Would you like to explain that a little more?*

Freire:

Yes. I think that first of all it is important to emphasise the impossibility of a neutral education because, in a general way and for the naive consciousness, it is not something obvious. It is impossible to have the neutrality of education just as it is impossible, for example, to have the neutrality of science. It means that no matter if we are conscious or not as educators, our praxis is either for the liberation of the people – their humanisation – or for their domestication, their domination. Precisely because of this I think it is very important to make clear the different forms of action in the field of education in order to make possible our true option or choice. If my choice is a liberating one, a humanising one, it is necessary for me to be absolutely clear concerning the methods, the techniques, the processes, which I have to use when I am before the educatees. Generally, we think that we are working for people, and that is with people, for their liberation, their humanisation; nevertheless we are using the same methods through which we prevent them from becoming free. This is so precisely because we are introjecting in ourselves the myths which we received in our experience in our schooling, and these myths are myths which

* This interview was first published in *RISK*, Vol. 6, No. 4, 1970, and is reprinted here with the kind permission of that journal's editor, Rex Davis, who is asking the questions. Emphasis is in the original.

57

make it impossible for us to develop a kind of action for freedom, for liberation. So it is not only necessary to know that it is impossible to have the neutrality of education, but it is absolutely necessary to define both these different and antagonistic actions. Thus, I need to analyse, *to know*, to distinguish these different ways in the field of education.

Risk:
Now, I think it is crucial for me to understand a little better what kinds of methods or actions, praxis, you see as liberating.

Freire:
Obviously, in order to answer this question I think that it is necessary to develop some reflections about, for example, the relationships between people and the reality of people in the world; or in other words, the relationships between consciousness and the world. This might seem to be a kind of escape from the concrete facts, and that would be a kind of metaphysics, but really it is not. Recently I wrote a paper for a meeting in Rome, in which I said that education for freedom, for liberation, must start from a kind of *archaeology of consciousness.*

Risk:
Would you like to explain a little more the phrase 'archaeology of consciousness'?

Freire:
First of all we don't have 'consciousness' here in the old term; that is, there is not this dichotomy between consciousness and the world. Second, 'consciousness' is not something, some empty space, within people. *Consciousness is intentionality towards the world.* When I think in this way of an archaeology of consciousness, I am thinking that through the problematisation of the relationships between human beings and the world, it is possible for them to recreate, to re-make, the natural process through which consciousness appeared in the process of his evolution, precisely in the moment which Teilhard de Chardin calls 'hominisation' in the evolution of humanity. When consciousness appears there is reflection; there is *intentionality towards the world.* Humanity becomes different, essentially

58

different, from animals. We can now not only know, but can know that we are knowing.

Risk:
Would you see any connection between this way of approaching the problem and, say, the Freudian insight about psychoanalysis – that to penetrate into one's unconsciousness is to discover oneself?

Freire:
From my point of view, education for freedom implies constantly, permanently, the exercise of consciousness turning in on itself in order to discover itself in the relationships with the world, trying to explain the reasons which can make clear the concrete situation people have in the world. But it is not enough. it is important to point out that reflection alone is not enough for the process of liberation. We need praxis or, in other words, we need to transform the reality in which we find ourselves. But in order to transform reality, in order to develop my action upon reality, transforming it, it is necessarily and constantly, the unity between my action and my reflection.

Risk:
Now, this is an integral part of your thinking. I wonder if we could move from the more sophisticated area of your philosophy to something in the way of your own praxis, the kinds of things you were involved in which may have helped you perceive this understanding.

Freire:
In the beginning of my experience in Brazil, many years ago, even though I exercised a critical reflection on my action in this process of looking for ways of working, it was possible for me to reflect again on my last 'reflection action': in order to theorise that 'reflection action'. So, first of all, I acted.

Risk:
Could you give an example?

Freire:
There is a very good example which I can give now. When I was thinking in Brazil concerning the possibility of developing a kind of method through which it was possible for illiterates to

learn how to read and write easily, I thought, in my library, when I was studying and reflecting – I thought – and I have never said this before – for the first time I am saying it – I thought that the best way was not to challenge the critical mind – the critical consciousness of people but (it is very interesting to note now the change which I made) . . . but to try to put into the consciousness of people some symbols associated with words without challenging their critical consciousness. And, in the second stage, to return and to challenge them critically in order to rediscover the association between certain symbols and the words, and so, to apprehend the words. And I remember that I invited an old woman, a very good woman – a peasant, illiterate – she worked with us in our home – she was a cook; and one Sunday I told her 'Look, Maria (that's her name) I am thinking to start a new way to help people who cannot read, how to read – and I need your help. Would you like to help me in this search?' She said, 'Yes'. And I invited her to my library, and I projected a picture with a boy and under this picture it was written in Portuguese *menino*, which is boy, and I asked her, 'Maria, what is this?' She said, '*Menino,* it's a boy, a *menino.*' I projected another picture with the same *menino* but orthographically the word *menino* without the middle syllable – so *meno* instead of *menino* – and I asked her, 'Maria, what is this?' She said, '*Menino,* again' and I asked her, 'Maria there is something missing?' And she said to me 'Oh yes, the middle is missing.' I smiled and I showed another picture with the same *menino*, but orthographically without the last syllable, *meni*, only *meni*, and I asked again, 'Is something missing?' 'Yes, the last piece of this.' We discussed, we talked, more or less 15 minutes with different situations with *menino, meno, nino, meni*, etc., and every time she captured the part, rather the lack of the part of the word, and she told me 'Look I am tired. It is very interesting but I am tired.' She was able to work really all the day, but nevertheless with ten or fifteen minutes of an intellectual exercise she became tired. It is normal. But she asked me, 'Do you think that I was able to help you?' I said, 'Yes. Yes you give me a great contribution. Because of you I have changed my way.' She said 'Thank you.' It is fantastic the capacity of love. And then she left my library and in five minutes more she came back with a cup of coffee for me.

60

Then immediately I stayed alone in my library, re-thinking my first hypothesis and I said to myself – now use your reflection on that last experience. I discovered that the way really would be to challenge from the beginning the intentionality of consciousness, that is the capacity of reflection of consciousness and not the other way in which I was thinking. So, I think that is a very good example, no? In order to demonstrate how to act and to reflect constantly and to change in the process of the search in which we are engaged. So with this simple example with Maria, I became convinced that the way would be another way, *I would have to challenge the critical consciousness from the beginning.*

Some days later, after this experience with Maria, I started with a group of five men, but this time challenging them in a critical way. When I told you before that it is necessary to try a kind of archaeology of consciousness, I don't want to say that it is necessary to invite people in order to discuss Chardin – in order to discuss the scientific dimensions of evolution! No, no, no! The archaeology of consciousness implies only to invite men and women who are at the naive level of their consciousness, ideologised in a concrete reality in which they cannot express themselves, they cannot express the word, they don't *know that they can know*! To invite them in order to discover that it is possible for them to know precisely because men and women can know that they are knowing.

Risk:
Now is this the process which is called conscientisation? Because this is a word which I think people don't quite understand.

Freire:
Yes, it is one of the dimensions of the *conscientizacao* process. And it is important also to underline this in order to understand what *conscientizacao* really is, it is necessary to avoid two kinds of mistakes into which we can fall. First, the mistake of idealism, the mistake of subjectivism, in which consciousness would be the creator of the world, that is of reality – we create a reality in our consciousness, consciousness creates the reality! The second mistake is a mistake in which we have only the objectivity, the hypertrophe of objectivity, which implies the objectivism that is the exacerbation of the power of objectivity in

creating or in conditioning consciousness. Consciousness appears in the relationships between people and the world, and reality. Nevertheless, it is not only the reflex of reality, because it is reflective. No? So, both of these mistakes cannot illuminate the process of *conscientizacao*.

Only when we understand the 'dialecticity' between consciousness and the world – that is, when we know that we don't have a consciousness here and the world there but, on the contrary, when both of them, the objectivity and the subjectivity, are incarnating dialectically, is it possible to understand what *conscientizacao* is, and to understand the role of consciousness in the liberation of humanity. I think that it is very important to emphasise this aspect, because many times people think that I am defending a kind of idealism, that I am here writing, thinking, saying, that people can liberate themselves in their consciousness yet it is impossible and I never said it. What I say is that if reflection itself alone is not enough for the process of the liberation of humanity, because we need action, so action itself alone cannot do it, precisely because human kind is not only action, but is also reflection.

Risk:
Does this mean that there must be a political dimension to the process of conscientisation? I would think that the people who are in the process of liberation, or discovering their liberated consciousness, can only continue the process at the same rate at which they involve themselves, commit themselves to the world.

Freire:
Yes, it is exactly what you are saying. In my point of view, we cannot liberate the others, people cannot liberate themselves alone, because people liberate themselves in communion, mediated by reality which they must transform. So, the process of liberation is not a gift which I give you. I think that the same thing concerns salvation, from the theological point of view.

Risk:
Tell me, in your experience now, how has some of your thinking been worked out? What are some of the examples of the praxis that you know of? Has there been any more development, or

have there been any other subtle changes that you know of, as the praxis has gone on?

Freire:

I think that it is very interesting to tell you of some changes in my praxis, not actually made by myself, but by other groups of young people and educators. For example, in Mexico, every year I go to Cuernavaca to give a seminar for Latin American groups. Last year [1969] in June I went there in order to co-ordinate a seminar for a week, with 150 people, more or less from Latin America. And last January I went there again, and I met a group of 15 people, young people, and ecumenical – because there were protestants and catholics in this group. After the seminar in June they created a group in order to begin work. And between June and January, when I went there again, they had a very good experience with results, objective results, and they told me, 'Look, Paulo, we would like to talk with you in order to show you something which we do differently to you.' And I said, 'Oh, fantastic'. And when they explained to me, they had made at least one thing differently to me, and I think that it is better than mine. I will tell you what was this dimension.

I said in my works, in my articles and books, that in the process of literacy, if your choice is a liberating and humanising one, we cannot start from our words, the generative words, but, on the contrary, we have to make a research with people in order to get their words. You have to start from the words of the people and not from your words – but they made something very, very good. Instead of making a search in order to discover the words of the people before a process of literacy, they started the process without the investigation! Now, how?

They proposed to the teams of illiterates some pictures, and I used also these pictures, in order to discuss precisely the relationships between people and the world in order to discover, for example, the difference between culture and nature, the action of people on reality, transforming reality, creating the world of men and women, which is the world of culture and history. And, through the discussion of the first picture, which they taped, they took the first word. That is, in discussing the first picture, which concerned the relationships between people and

63

reality, they took the first generative word from the people. And the second day they discussed the first generative word, without knowing the second. In the discussion of the first generative word they captured the second word and so on.

Risk:
Now, when you use the phrase 'generative word' you are describing obviously a particular word. Would you give me an example of what a generative word is?

Freire:
Yes. In a syllabic language, like Portuguese or Spanish for instance, the generative words are those which, being composed in syllables, make possible through the combination of these syllables the creation of other words. For example, you have in Spanish the word *paloma* – the bird of peace, a dove. If you break up this word *paloma* is *pa, pe, pi, po, pu*; the family of the second is *la, le, li, lo, lu*; called a linguistic family. That is the family of the first syllable of *paloma* is *pa, pe, pi, po, pu*; the family of the second is *la, le, li, lo, lu*; and the third is *ma, me, mi, mo, mu.* After the breaking up of this word into its syllables, you have the three linguistic families – and now you can create words through new combinations, in this case I think it is more or less eighty words, no? And precisely because these illiterates are not orally illiterate (you understand men can be illiterate and yet speak, talk in their language) so they can recognise new words in the combinations, and in the possibility of combining these syllables, they can recognise their vocabulary – and so they recreate their vocabulary.

But the question with this team of Mexicans was that I started investigating the seventeen generative words which are necessary in Spanish or Portuguese for the process of literacy, before the process itself. They started from the discussion of people in the world and through the discussion they captured a generative word. And I think that it is very important, in certain regions above all, in which people are not believing any more and are tired – it is very important to start with people immediately the process of literacy – and through these initial discussions it is possible to capture the words of people.

64

Risk:

Now, what do you think about the problem of schooling? Coming back to this original idea that you had that there can be education for liberation and education which is for domestication, where do you see the school? Most people would argue that, well, the school system is where we combat illiteracy, yet it is a very expensive way. Is it possible that the method you are talking about is a choice, an option, in this problem of literacy?

Freire:

I see. Look, for example, in Brazil when we were working at the national level – I don't remember just now precisely the cost of each educational unit – but it was very, very, very accessible for an underdeveloped country like Brazil. I remember that the projector which we imported from Poland cost $2.50, bought in Brazil, and the strip film $1 more or less for an educational unit. I think that in total, each unit for the literacy process was around $5, or $6-$7 more or less. But in two months you have, in each unit, 25 people reading, using the same material, so in four months, with 50 people reading, the cost disappears.

Risk:

You certainly reveal the cost of your method. I take it that you have a team of illiterate people and you work with them for about eight weeks, and using your method of discovering words through pictures, and through talking about the generative word and how this grows – that in eight weeks you will achieve a certain level of literacy which I take it then is sufficient, a kind of take-off point?

Freire:
Yes, only this.

Risk:

So that in eight week periods you can achieve this take-off with adult illiterate people, but a child, going through to reach the same level of literacy would take so many years in an expensive school system, so that comparison in expense alone, in cost analysis, is in favour of your literacy programme.

Freire:
Yes, I think so, yes.

Risk:
But you would have other objections to schools, beside the cost element, surely?

Freire:
Yes. Look, I think that Ivan Illich is absolutely right when he describes the schools, no matter their levels – primary or not – as instruments of social control. Really, schools themselves are domesticating institutions. I don't know whether you know a very beautiful song by Tom Paxton, I think, and the song is sung by Pete Seeger, in which he asks the little boy, 'What did you learn today in school, little boy of mine?' I think that the answer which the boy gives in this song would be, with some differences, the same answer which millions and millions of children would give today in the world. That is, a school itself builds the alienation of us, in us, precisely because the task of schools – in a wrong way . . . in a wrong perception – is to transfer to the students the existing knowledge.

But look – it is very, very important to note – the existing knowledge exists because consciousness, in its reflective power, can know. A person as a conscious body can not only know the existing knowledge, but can know new knowledge, or can make new knowledge. Really, the existing knowledge today was born from the knowledge of yesterday, which became old; as well, future knowledge must be born from the existing knowledge of today. That is, *knowledge is a process.* But what does the school mean? It is a house in which the students are invited to assume a passive attitude in order to receive the transference of the existing knowledge without reflection on the very possibility of the creation of this knowledge! I don't know if I am very clear. It is because of this I talked before of the archaeology of consciousness.

Instead of transferring the existing knowledge it is necessary to invite consciousness to assume the active attitude without which it is impossible to create knowledge. But this is not happening in the primary school . . . in the university it is the same thing – and it implies a mythologisation of reality, because only education for liberation implies demythologising reality, while education for domestication implies mythologising reality, no? It is very interesting, no? But it is not possible for the power elites, for example, to prevent people from thinking. Okay? It is impossible. It is impossible because to think – thinking – results from our relationships with the world and because we became, in our process of evolution, reflective beings. So it is impossible to prevent people from thinking. But if it is not possible to prevent people from thinking, it is necessary, in order to maintain the status quo, to mythologise reality, in order to mythologise consciousness. Because it would be impossible also to falsify reality without falsifying consciousness, because reality is a reality of consciousness, so it is necessary to falsify the consciousness of reality. So – the falsification of reality is itself the falsification of consciousness, and, because of this, it is necessary to use propaganda – the more you are falsifying reality – mythologising reality – you are mythologising the consciousness of men and women.

People live by myths, and people are involved in myths and not in the truth, but having the illusion that they are thinking correctly. Education for liberation, on the contrary, has to demythologise reality in order to demythologise consciousness and because of this, I repeat, I talked about the archaeology of consciousness; and in the education for domestication we have another kind of archaeology, it would be the 'archaeology of irrationality'.

Risk:
You have marvellous phrases! . . . You see, implicit in what you are saying in challenging the schools as being what Illich calls instruments of social control is surely a very direct challenge to the churches, because they are equally instruments of social control. Not only because they maintain a number of schools, in fact historically they have played a large part in creating the kind of school system which is now being sacralised throughout society, but they themselves still persevere, I should think, in this kind of mythologising of reality. Now, what would you say about the churches in this context?

Freire:
Recently I wrote a letter answering another one to a young American theologian in which I said something about this. I

67

think that the real role of the church should not be the role of mythologising, the role of domestication, the role of developing the bureaucracy of faith.

Risk:
Exactly.

Freire:
In my point of view, on the contrary, the role of the church must be the role of liberation, of the humanisation of human-kind . . . Precisely because of this I am more and more interested in working with theologians. In my point of view theology today has many things to do. That is, from my point of view theology is not something superfluous. No, on the contrary. But it is obvious, I don't mean a false theology, not a theology of 'bla, bla, bla' – idealistic theology – but a theology which is part of anthropology, which is engaged historically in order to discuss, for example, the word of God, and our relations with the very word of God. I think that my attitude cannot be the attitude of an empty being waiting to be filled by the word of God. I think also that in order to listen to it, it is necessary for me to be engaged in the process of the liberation of humanity. Because of this I think that theology, such a theology should be connected with education for liberation – and education for liberation with theology.

I am very interested, and I am thinking for example, to make it possible next year – not necessarily through the World Council of Churches – to have a meeting in Geneva with some catholic and protestant theologians of the third world (not geographically speaking, but the third world of the first world, also) in order to discuss this kind of theology – it is a great pre-occupation today in Latin America. We have between the protestants and between the catholics a preoccupation with such a theology.

Finally, I think that our task as christians cannot be a paternalistic one. That is, I cannot be author of your salvation. I cannot leave my home in order to look for sinners to save them. I have to live as a man among men and women! – discussing, acting, transforming, creating – and in all the dimensions of my life, my existence, I can find the presence of God, but the

68

presence of God does not mean the imposition of God. God is a presence – nevertheless, this presence does not prevent myself from making history, that is the history of the liberation of humanity.

Risk:
Perhaps the theology of liberation and the liberation of humanity may well be ultimately the liberation of God.

Freire:
Yes, because God, too, in a certain way, is mythologised by us.

5. Freire, Praxis and Education
by Reginald Connolly

The importance of Paulo Freire lies in the emphasis he gives to the hitherto ignored political nature of education. He sees significant implications in this regard, not only for the third but also for the first world. His thinking demonstrates the power of education as a liberating force. To achieve this however, the oppressed require their own pedagogy. It is through offering other models for teaching and learning that Freire produces radical alternatives to the existing narrative forms of education. He believes that neutrality always conceals a choice. There can be no neutrality in human praxis, and so education is either for domestication or for liberation. If it is for liberation then the very methods and techniques in use for domestication must be inappropriate. Furthermore, he has illustrated most convincingly that pedagogy can no longer be imprisoned in the confines of the school. Its task is to unveil its own political options, to define itself in relation to the productive forces, the political power structure, and the dominant ideology of any given society. Not only in the universities, but also in secondary and primary schools, education is always a political event. Power is inseparable from education. Those who hold power define what education will be, its methods, programmes and curriculum.

Where the learner is defined as a passive object, a context is created wherein he or she becomes not only dependent, but also mute in the face of superior knowledge and power. This is the predicament of the culture of silence in which large numbers of people become trapped in an ignorance defined and imposed by others. Within such a context it is impossible for the dispossessed, who are forced to mimic the dictates of their paternal overlords, to have authentic voices of their own. It is important to realise however that silence does not signify an absence of response, but rather a response which lacks a critical quality. The

70

entire educative process, Freire suggests, is a major instrument for maintaining the culture of silence.

Conscientisation does not occur automatically. It comes mainly from a critical educational effort based on favourable historical conditions. It has to do with the process in which the oppressed, not as recipients but as knowing subjects, achieve a deepening awareness both of the socio-cultural reality which shapes their lives, and their capacity to transform it. Conscientisation seeks the awakening of critical consciousness, and results in the identification and naming of social ills which constitute oppressive circumstances. The fragmented consciousness suffered by the oppressed denies them access to each other in their collaborative search for a picture of their total situation. Maintaining fragmentation is always in the interests of the oppressor. Where fragmentation of consciousness gives place to collaboration through dialogue, revolution is invited. On this Freire says,

> because men are historical beings, incomplete and conscious of being incomplete, revolution is as natural and permanent a human dimension as is education.[1]

So the process of conscientisation has a significant political dimension to it. People who are in the process of liberation, or are discovering their liberated consciousness, can only continue the process when they commit themselves to the world. Conscientisation is much more than a simple process of increasing awareness. It is essentially geared to the radical transformation of social reality.

Writing in the introduction to *Education: the Practice of Freedom*, Denis Goulet has observed that:

> Freire is no ethnocentric reductionist: he knows that action without critical reflection and even without gratuitous contemplation is disastrous activism. Conversely, he insists that theory or introspection in the absence of collective social action is escapist idealism or wishful thinking. In his view, genuine theory can only be derived from some *praxis* rooted in historical struggles.[2]

Objective social reality neither exists nor can be transformed by

71

mere chance, because both are the results of human action. Because the social reality is produced by human beings and conditions them, transforming this conditioning is an historical task which also must be performed by them. One of the main obstacles to the achievement of liberation is that oppressive reality absorbs those within it and thus stifles the emergence of critical consciousness. Oppression is functionally domesticating. If one is to escape, one must emerge from it and turn upon it. This can only be done by praxis: reflection and action upon the world in order to transform it.

The oppressed only begin to have faith in themselves when they unmask the oppressor and work for their liberation through organised struggle. Such a revelation cannot be solely intellectual, it must also involve action. The oppressed must be able to view themselves as being engaged in the ontological and historical vocation of becoming more fully human. True reflection must entail action, and action will constitute an authentic praxis only if its results are subjected to critical reflection. Without conscious and concomitant involvement, action is nothing more than pure activism. Freire's pedagogy of the oppressed requires dialogue, reflection and communication to encompass this praxis: slogans, communiques, monologues and lectures will vitiate it. Since knowledge results from invention and re-invention, learning cannot truly take place apart from enquiry, apart from praxis. In this way, praxis leads the oppressed from naive fatalistic acceptance of reality, to a perception of its causes. This shift in consciousness is confirmed by subsequent intervention.

For Paulo Freire education is a relation between subjects in the act of knowing. It is mediated by the object to be known, and by the educator continually reconstructing this act of knowing. It is, therefore, problem-posing. The task of the educator is to present the subject as a problem, the content of which mediates it, and not to discourse on it, extend it, or hand it over, as if it were a matter of something already done, constituted, completed, and finished. In this process no one can present something to someone else as a problem, while at the same time remaining a mere spectator.

In problem-posing education the teacher's role does not

shift from cognitive to narrative. It is always cognitive whether in preparing lesson notes or in dialogue with students. By treating cognisable objects, not as deposits to be handed out to students, but as ideas for critical reflection, both students and teacher become critical co-investigators in dialogue with each other. Thus the teacher's own opinions and views are constantly being acted upon by the discussion and expressions of students. In this way both students and teacher find themselves challenged, and feel obliged to meet the challenge, because it is not offered in an isolated vacuum, but presented in a total context, connected with other living situations. Action is stimulated over and above simple reflection, and learners begin to perceive critically the way in which they exist in the world with which, and in which, they find themselves. Their perception of the world thus alters. Instead of seeing reality as static, it becomes living and transformable.

It is important to observe how Freire distinguishes between problem-solving and problem-posing methods of education. 'Problem-solving' is a ubiquitous feature of most current education programmes. Selected, isolated problems are often presented to students entirely at the whim and choosing of the teacher, irrespective of their relevance to the actual, or perceived reality of students. The situations so presented are often highly artificial and divorced from the real world. Added to these highly contrived circumstances is the fact that one cut and dried solution to the problem is usually posited. But life is not like that at all. Many problems co-exist. They have a universal field in which they are related and co-related with other problem situations: one cut and dried solution is seldom possible. Often, problems are not solved, only a better understanding of their nature may be possible. 'Problem-solving' thus objectifies reality, analyses it into component parts, devises means for solving difficulties in the most efficient way, and then dictates a strategy or policy. Freire believes that 'problem-solving' only serves to distort the totality of human experience, by reducing it to those dimensions which are amenable to treatment.

When education and especially schooling become acts of depositing, with the students as the depositories and the teacher as the depositor, we see Freire's famous 'banking concept of education' in operation. Communication gives way to communiques by the teacher, who makes deposits which the students meekly receive, memorise and repeat. Their field of action does not exceed the acts of receiving, filing and storing away the deposits, becoming collectors or cataloguers of the things they store. In the end, it is the students themselves who are filed away.

Freire is uncompromising in repudiating this filling of human consciousness with the food of facts. The metaphor of the bread of the spirit nourishing the marginal man is further extended to include the poison herb of illiteracy which causes disease. Small wonder that Sartre was moved to exclaim, *'O philosophie alimentaire!'* when contemplating this predominantly digestive concept of education. For Freire, education is afflicted with narration sickness, a significant feature of which is the sonority of words, not their transforming power. He states as an example, 'Four times four is sixteen', 'the capital of Para is Belem'. Students record, memorise and repeat the phrases without perceiving what four times four really means, or actually realising the true significance of 'capital', that is what Belem means for Para, and what Para means for Brazil. The banking concept projects absolute ignorance on to others, by means of deposits in the form of slogans, communiques, monologues, and lectures, in the place of fruitful dialogue. Education for domination stimulates the credulity of students with the ideological intent of indoctrinating them to adapt to the ideology of oppression.

Freire suggests that dialogue is the principal means by which the banking concept can be opposed. Dialogue characterises the act of knowing. The cognitive act of dialogue occurs when what is to be known is grasped by those who seek to know it, and surrenders itself as mediator between two seekers in their critical unveiling of the object to be known. Freire urges us to consider the epistemological cycle as a totality, and to refrain from separating the stage of gaining existing knowledge from the stage of discovering and creating new knowledge. In both these stages, the subjects who desire to know must face the objects of their knowledge from the stage of discovering and creating new knowledge. In both these stages, the subjects who desire to know

74

must face the objects of their knowledge with a critical and curious approach. If the critical approach is invalidated through a lapse in the dialogical relationship, mere transference of knowledge occurs. 'To know' becomes no longer a creative or recreative act but merely a digestive act. Freire insists that the teacher is not merely the one who teaches, but is also the one who is taught in dialogue with students. The students in this complementary dialectical relationship while being taught also teach the teacher. Teacher and students co-operate in an activity in which all of them grow. Authoritarianism has no place in a dialogical situation. As the teacher dialogues with students their attention must be drawn to matters that are unclear. The approach must always be problematic asking, Why?, How?, Is this true? What is the relation between what you have just said and what the person before you said? Do you think there is any difference between these two statements? Why? It is superfluous to say that such an approach is time consuming, that there is a curriculum to be completed. There is nothing which cannot be presented problematically.

Freire's approach here involves thematics or the investigation of how people think. For him this is the thinking that occurs when the oppressed seek to understand their reality together. It is not possible to think for others, or without others. Nor can others think for us. Every thematic investigation which deepens historical awareness is truly educational. All authentic education enquires into thinking. The more teachers investigate their students' thinking, and are thus jointly educated, the more they continue to investigate. Thematic investigation and problem-posing education are not to be separated, they are simply different moments of the same process.

Freire quotes the results of a thematic investigation carried out among a group of slum residents in Santiago. A scene was projected for the culture circle depicting a drunk staggering down the street and three young men on the street corner conversing. If the usual type of study on the effects of alcoholism had been intended and the usual type of questionnaire issued, the participants would almost certainly have criticised the drunken man adversely, as they were expected to. But the scene they were decoding was something which was part of their own concrete reality, and their response, though perhaps surprising, was very different to that anticipated. They suggested the drunk was the only one in that group of four who was truly productive and useful to his community. He had probably been returning home after working a very long day on a miserably low wage, and he was deeply worried because on that wage he was unable to care for his family. He was the only one among the four who actually worked. He was a decent worker, but frustrated, and so a drunk.

Explaining Freire's use of thematics Manfred Stanley says:

> The first stage is 'thematic' investigation by which Freire apparently means intelligently conceived and executed anthropological research on the objective situation and the phenomenal world of the illiterate group being worked with . . . Together, always in dialogical manner, educators and learners move through the literacy materials (words, texts, pictures) gradually 'de-coding' them.[3]

Each historical period is characterised by a series of aspirations, concerns and values. The concrete representation of these, as well as the obstacles to their fulfilment, constitute the themes of that epoch, which in turn indicate the tasks to be carried out. The complex of interacting themes of an epoch constitutes its thematic universe.

Freire's anthropological concept of culture highlights the distinction between the world of nature, and the world of culture. Culture is the addition made by people to a world they did not make. It is the result of their own labour, their efforts to create and re-create. It is the systematic acquisition of human experience as creative assimilation, not as information-storing. As such, it helps the illiterate uncover the realisation that popular songs are no less culture than the poetry of learned poets. Freire is confident that culture, discussed imaginatively in all of its dimensions, can provide the foundation of the search for knowledge.

Every educational situation implies a theory of knowledge put into practice. Yet in education we often do what Freire describes as a 'terrible thing'. We dichotomise existing knowledge and the knowing act, that is we separate the possession of knowledge from the act of creating knowledge. Schools thus

76

become repositories for the extension of knowledge, with the teachers as its possessors and guardians. Freire emphasises the social character of an act of knowing. Whatever the level, knowing is not the act by which a learner is transformed into an object, who meekly adapts to the contents given or imposed by someone else. Instead, it requires the curious presence of subjects confronting the world. It demands transforming action on reality, constant searching, invention and re-invention. In the learning situation the only person who actually learns is the person who is capable of appropriating the experience into his or her own concrete existential circumstances. An act of knowing then, must comprise an authentic dialogue between teacher and students. Both are subject subjects in the exercise, united together in the cognition of a knowable object which mediates between them. Both must be engaged in the constant problematisation of their existential situation. However, where teachers are obsessed with the trading of facts as merchandise, they will fail to explore the breadth and width of intellectual speculation. In the classroom there should be more concern with causes than with effects in discussions of all aspects of knowledge.

Freire develops this approach to knowing by analysing dialogue as a human phenomenon. The quintessence of dialogue is the word, which is more than the spoken or written unit of communication. For Freire the word has two components or two dimensions: reflection and action. Whenever these two constituent elements are separated the word degenerates either into mere verbalism, or rash activism. The traditional curriculum, Freire says is based on words divorced from the reality that they are meant to signify, and thus becomes merely alienating 'blah'. He continues:

> In most reading programmes, the students must endure an abysm between their own experience and the contents offered for them to learn. It requires patience indeed, after the hardships of a day's work (or of a day without work) to tolerate lessons dealing with 'wing'. 'Johnny saw the wing.' 'The wing is on the bird.' Lessons talking of Graces and grapes to men who never knew a Grace and never ate a grape. 'Grace saw the grape!'[4]

But teaching literacy is not a matter of mouthing and memorising words like 'strand', 'grand', 'brand', 'land', and 'hand', thus keeping reality opaque, and dulling the consciousness of the learner with innumerable alienating words and phrases. On the contrary, teaching is an apprenticeship in naming the world. The teacher must focus on the vocabular universe of students, and relate speaking the word to transforming reality. Codification was used in Freire's culture circles to isolate and identify a significant element in the learner's existential situation, and to problematise the resultant word. Words not vitally and intimately connected with the learners' existence were rejected. Words were no longer magical, they assumed new power as illiterates discovered themselves, and their potential, and began to name things around them. In the process adult illiterates not only learned words but became critically conscious of their social framework. *'Favela'* in Recife or Rio de Janeiro, and *'callampa'* in Chile, represented the social, economic and cultural reality of the people – the slums which were so much a part of their lives.

Fundamental to Freire's pedagogy is the resolution of the teacher-student contradiction. This is because education, over and above seeking literacy, must embody critical dialogue including action. Reflective participation and not monologue is required. The teacher who strives to achieve praxis must have faith in students, and trust in their power to reason and reflect. Freire cites ten ways in which the teacher-student contradiction is manifest:

(i) The teacher teaches and the students are taught.
(ii) The teacher knows everything and the students know nothing.
(iii) The teacher thinks and the students are thought about.
(iv) The teacher talks and the students listen – meekly.
(v) The teacher disciplines and the students are disciplined.
(vi) The teacher chooses and enforces his choice, and the students comply.
(vii) The teacher acts and the students have the illusion of acting through the action of the teacher.

78

(viii) The teacher chooses the programme content, and the students comply.

(ix) The teacher confuses the authority of knowledge with his own professional authority, which he sets in opposition to the freedom of the students.

(x) The teacher is the subject of the learning process, while the pupils are mere objects.[5]

In opposition to this banking model of education, Freire insists that liberating pedagogy consists in acts of cognition, not the transfer of information. Depositing in the classroom must give way to problem-posing, so that students are required to examine, to know, and to transform their world, and thus participate in genuine communication. Yet in the normal teaching situation the teacher prepares, learns, makes notes, or otherwise masters his topic, working in the library, laboratory, study or wherever else he can find material. Freire cites as an example the case of a study of Socrates, a topic with which he was familiar from his own university teaching experience. The dedicated teacher very thoroughly digests a considerable corpus of information on Socrates and then regurgitates it to his students who are only too eager to devour his words. There is much 'existing' knowledge on Socrates; for example, his teachings, his concept of dialogue and the historical details of his life.

Freire suggests that there are two ways in which we could approach the task of understanding Socrates. We could spend two or three months of the course giving lessons and explanations about what Socrates did, without establishing any relationship between Socrates and his times, Socrates and his society, Socrates and the challenges he faced. What were the circumstances that led Socrates to arrive at his way of thinking? In fact, why did he think in the way he did? Or we could challenge our students to think on the concrete reality which made it possible for such a man as Socrates to make his appearance. Like ourselves, he too was a being in history, conditioned, and shaped, by his historical circumstances. Furthermore, he belonged to a particular class in Athenian democracy during that particular period of Greek history. Clearly it is the latter approach that Freire favours because it fosters critical reflection on the object

79

of knowledge, in this case Socrates. This is because it poses Socrates as a problem requiring joint investigation by teacher and student. In the former approach Socrates becomes the teacher's private property, to be dispensed, according to whim, in large or small doses.

When considering curriculum Freire's work poses a significant critique of traditional perspectives, which posit a notion of knowledge as external to the student. This implies that the teacher merely initiates or inducts the passive student into tacitly agreed worthwhile activities, skills and knowledge. In this way the traditional curriculum resembles an ivory tower of ideas. Where the choice of direction falls exclusively on the educator, it accordingly takes a vertical, donating form from the very outset. But if the dialectics of education are considered it becomes obvious that if the curriculum is to be relevant, we need a preliminary knowledge of the aspirations, levels of perception, and the view of the world which our students take. This knowledge should be the starting point for a curriculum. However, it will not do merely to discourse on the current situation. If we do, we run the risk of adapting to the banking concept of education. Moreover, teachers must be aware that if they are not understood it could be because their language is out of tune with the concrete situation of their students. Freire stresses that the language of the teacher cannot exist without thought, and thought and language cannot exist without a structure to which they refer. Effective communication therefore demands an understanding of the structural conditions in which the thought and language of the students are dialectically framed. It is imperative to frame our curriculum accordingly. We must go to the 'thematic universe' of our students for the complex of generative themes we need if we are to find the proper content for the curriculum.

Thematic investigation is a common striving towards awareness of reality and self, thus making it a starting point for the whole educational process. In searching for relevant themes teachers should be acutely aware of the need to study the interconnection between possible themes and the need to pose them as problems in an historical and cultural context. Freire found the anthropological concept of culture a basic theme around which his educational programme could be organised. He is convinced that educators cannot present their own curriculum, but must seek for it dialogically with the learners. If we are to adopt methods which foster dialogue and reciprocity, we must be committed to equality and the abolition of privilege. It is impossible to think about a methodology which is neutral. It will always be determined by politics. The ruling class in society not only define the content of education, they also prescribe its methodology. So the liberating pedagogy Freire advocates logically entails the revolutionary transformation of class society. In highlighting the political nature of education, and the praxis this necessarily involves, Freire is providing a framework for the humanisation of all.

6. Knowledge, Action and Power
by Michael Matthews

An educator without an epistemology is like a sailor without a rudder – blown around by whatever fads, fashions and ideologies dominate the current educational scene. Paulo Freire's theory of knowledge is central to his pedagogy. Thankfully, unlike many educationalists who construct an epistemology in vacuo and then propose it as a guide to teaching, Freire's epistemology itself emerges out of the process of reflection upon his own experiences in knowledge transmission and acquisition; out of education in catholic action groups, in cultural circles, in revolutionary cells, in the enormous task of creating literacy and understanding in a country kept ignorant and silent by centuries of Portuguese colonisation.

In a theory of knowledge we expect to find opinions on questions such as: what are the personal and social factors which facilitate the development of understanding? What methods are conducive to the creation of knowledge? What are the procedures whereby we can identify mistaken and inadequate cognitions of the natural and social world? How do politics and interests manifest themselves in the corpus of public knowledge any society delineates and into which it systematically introduces people? These are questions addressed by Freire. And yet Freire is not a systematic philosopher. Nor is he a sophisticated economist, sociologist, marxologist, psychologist or theologian. His epistemology is perhaps the best developed part of his theory, but even here we look in vain for a detailed, elaborated and defended position. Rather we have scattered comments, analyses, allusions and reflections. My argument here is that his epistemology is the same as that of the young Marx – the Marx of the *Paris Manuscripts* and the *Theses on Feuerbach* – and that it shares all the strengths and some of the weaknesses of these early reflections of Marx. Whatever the technical and other deficien-

82

cies of his position are, Freire is well in front of positivists and idealists who have alternately mesmerised teachers. These have proposed apolitical, non-practical, privatised accounts of human knowledge. Against these Freire asserts that knowledge comes out of reflecting upon the actions and engagements that restless, questioning, active subjects participate in when they transform their natural and social world. Knowledge is intimately linked with praxis. Such praxis itself is social, and is directed towards an end – human liberation and the emancipation of those trapped in a culture of silence. Thus public knowledge will be an arena within which political battles must be fought and ethical choices exercised. Whether labour history or constitutional history is taught in a university reflects a political decision; whether heart transplant knowledge is developed and transmitted, or medical knowledge concerned with non-drug intensive treatment of common diseases, is also a political decision.

Aspects of Freire's Epistemology

Agency, or the ability to act and intervene, is cited constantly by Freire as a precondition for the acquisition of knowledge. 'Knowing', he writes, 'is the task of subjects, not of objects.'[1] This connects him with an experimental tradition in philosophy, a tradition in which Hegel, Marx and Dewey are to be found. It opposes him to forms of both rationalism and empiricism which entertain inertness, passivity or aloofness as the correct disposition for intellectual mastery of the world. This tradition discounts labour, activity and manipulation as having no epistemological significance. It can be seen in Plato, in Augustine, and in the Chinese mandarins who cultivated inordinately long fingernails to provide a visible testament to their distance from manual work. The view that knowledge is best acquired by inert objects is vividly embodied in the person of Mr Gradgrind, the austere school teacher in Charles Dickens's *Hard Times*. He has his pupils lined up in serial ranks, and stands over them saying that they will have nothing in their heads but facts and that he will root out everything but the facts. To question, or to have an opinion is subversive of the learning process. In Freire's terms this is 'banking education', where pupils are reduced to passive receptacles for teacher transmitted deposits.

Galileo's achievements can be understood as the triumph of agency over passivity in science. The Aristotelians were very keen observers; they were the empiricists of their day, but they were not experimenters, manipulators, actors. They stood before nature and observed and recorded. Galileo intervened in nature; his experiments involved delimiting and controlling specific natural processes, and then manipulating discrete variables in the situation. Speaking figuratively, Galileo realised that nature had to be tortured in order to reveal her secrets. Scientific experimentation is predicated upon the assumption that to know nature we must act on it; that knowledge is created by subjects, not by objects.

But activity presupposes material and psychological necessities. In situations of oppression these are denied the oppressed groups: meetings are banned; funds are not available; technologies and information are limited and so on. Beyond these, people who are brought up to devalue themselves and their culture, to internalise a slave mentality, are going to lack the sense of being capable and in control. Action, intervention and manipulation are material realities which ultimately depend upon varying degrees of power for their exercise. This dialectic of bettering material circumstances, then action of some kind, followed by expanded consciousness, followed by power, followed by further expansion of material circumstances is a common enough pattern in all liberation movements. During the Algerian uprising, Arab women were pressed into service to carry arms and the like. As the French clamped down more and more on men, the sphere of activity of women increased. Against the desires of their men, historical necessities brought the women out of their kitchens and bedrooms into meetings and battles. Concomitant with this was a change in consciousness, a growing sense of themselves as subjects. Thus when the political revolution was won, Arab men had to confront the unpleasant fact that there had been a domestic revolution. The experience of subjectness had transformed the consciousness of the women: they were not going back to the old ways.

Praxis presupposes philosophical realism. For Freire there

84

is a world independent of people, a world which is the object of our intellectual conceptualisation. Freire is opposed to idealism, where the real is dissolved in the interests of subjectivity. He is not a Bishop Berkeley, for whom to exist is to be seen to exist. Ontologically, consciousness and the real are distinct. What Freire and Marx both recognise though, is that the world is always a world *for* people. Our intellectual comprehension of the world is determined by our needs and our interests. We do not just catalogue an alien and objective world, we come to know it in as much as it satisfies our needs and suits our interests. Geometry begins in Egypt as an aid to reclamation of the periodically flooded Nile valley; astronomy begins as an aid to navigation; Galileo commended his new science to merchants and military figures; the California Institute of Technology was founded explicitly for the purpose of solving scientific problems confronting American industry. It is interests and politics which mediate between human consciousness and a world which exists independently of that consciousness. This link is unfortunately overlooked in many realist accounts of the relationship of consciousness and world.

Human beings bring into being another reality as they live in, and intellectually appropriate, the world. At one level this is the reality of artefacts, of the built and planned environment, of ordered agriculture. It is what Marx referred to as 'humanised nature': the nature we see when we look over rural farmlands or urban landscapes. For Hegel this created world represents the beginnings of self-consciousness. Subjects come to know themselves as they externalise themselves in objects; as they materialise and embody their conceptions and ideas. At another level this created reality is the reality of human culture: of language; of institutions; of myths; of religions; of accumulated public knowledge. Freire is insistent that both levels of created reality become the object of people's knowledge, so that we can recognise its 'conditioning power'.[3]

Freire is recognising what many philosophers now acknowledge – that there is no eyeball to eyeball confrontation between a knowing subject and the world. As one prominent philosopher of science has said 'there is more to seeing than meets the eyeball'.[4] Our knowledge is a function of what is in the world plus what we bring to the world. Copernicus made a similar point with respect to how we perceive planetary motion – it is a mixture of two motions, the planets and the viewing subjects. It was not for nothing that Kant referred to his own contribution to philosophy as a 'Copernican revolution'. his basic anti-empiricist insight was correct – the mind has an active and constitutive role to play in conceptualising the world. Further, there is no escaping this fact. Kant was correct on this. Where he was incorrect, and where Marx and Freire are correct, is that he saw the structures of mind in innate, ahistorical and asocial terms: his famous categories, that together with sense impressions, determined experience. This is inadequate. It is created theories, public conceptions, common understanding that feed into, and are constitutive of, the way individuals experience the world. These things are historical, not innate and universal. As Freire says, they do have a conditioning power, and this has to be scrutinised, recognised and tested.

Freire recognises the necessarily social nature of thought. In places he expressed this enigmatically as 'the we think determines the I think'.[5] Once more he is in opposition to privatised and individualised epistemologies which take as their point of departure an individual confronting the world and proceeding to intellectually appropriate it. These are Robinson Crusoe models, perhaps epitomised by John Locke's ahistoric, individualist, tabula rasa theory of mind. The empiricist tradition, right down to twentieth century sense-data theorists have maintained versions of this asocial theory of knowledge. Marx in his 1844 manuscripts warned against establishing 'society' as an abstraction vis-à-vis the individual. He was insistent in saying that the individual is a social being. This is an Hegelian insight. We see it surfacing in the opening pages of Karl Mannheim's important book *Ideology and Utopia*, a work which had a significant influence on Freire. There Mannheim points out that strictly speaking it is incorrect to say that the single individual thinks. Rather, it is more correct to insist that he participates in thinking further what other men have thought before him. Thus Freire is correct in saying that the 'I think is enhanced if the we think is enhanced'. This is an epistemological basis for dialogue, for sharing ideas and analyses, for openness and for a positive

86

approach to making as rich as possible one's own intellectual and social milieu. This truth is in sharp contradiction to the privatised practice of so much of our educational system. Essays are written alone, students are pitted against students, examinations are tests of individual performance and so on.

It is the understanding that thought is social which enables us to appreciate why Freire's central notion of 'conscientisation' is not equivalent to enlightenment. The former arises out of public, social practices; the latter is often taken to depend upon private, reflective isolation. Because conscientisation occurs among real men and women, who live in real social structures, Freire correctly says that 'it cannot remain on the level of the individual'.[6]

The thesis that consciousness is social has many implications for epistemology, yet we look in vain to Freire for the elaboration of these. Fortunately, the thesis is elaborated and defended elsewhere. Indeed much contemporary anti-empiricist writing in epistemology and philosophy of science is preoccupied with giving accounts of the frameworks with which our observations are made and our theories formulated. Ludwig Wittgenstein's arguments against the possibility of private language, Thomas Kuhn's work on the function of paradigms in science, Stephen Toulmin's account of conceptual populations are all witness to the richness and heuristic worth of the thesis Freire enunciates. Unfortunately many psychologists studying concept acquisition and the like have ignored it. The most notable of these is Jean Piaget's Kantian interpretation, which leaves aside societies and histories as factors in the development of mind.

To stress the social dimension of knowledge is to draw attention to the possibility of ignorance. Communities may lack the concepts and theories that enable correct understanding. This is the problem of ideology. There can be communal flights from understanding in which the individual is a participant. These flights take off from a material base, they do not have solely an intellectual impetus. Misunderstanding can be ingrained in the texture of a society and systematically inculcated in its school system. Mao Tse-tung in his essay 'On practice' reiterates Marx's view that ideologies and flights from understanding are class-based: in a class society everyone lives as a member of a particular class, and every kind of thinking, without exception, is stamped with the brand of class.[7]

Hence Freire's remark that middle-class catholics in Recife were defending their class rather than their faith, and that their class position prevented them being converted to the people. Individuals not only live in society, but society also lives in individuals. Thus Freire's concern in Brazil, and in Guinea-Bissau, to bring into scrutiny the innumerable ways in which metropolitan culture was imposed upon the life and minds of the colonised.

Knowledge involves abstraction from experience. In the process of reflecting upon experience we abstract, and thus create the framework for comprehending the world and our experience of it:

> For learners to know what they did not know before, they must engage in an authentic process of abstraction by means of which they can reflect on the action-object whole.[8]

Freire is not a naive empiricist or a sensualist. Knowledge does not come from people simply having sense stimulation. Marx, in the *Grundrisse*, speaks about thought appropriating the concrete in terms of the abstract. The world, as it is conveyed and verbalised, is a world composed of abstractions and demarcated by concepts. What Freire is stressing here is the active part the mind plays in knowledge acquisition. This is a point overlooked by nearly all advocates of discovery learning. People never simply see, or simply experience, or simply discover. They always see, experience, and discover particular things depending upon what is already in their heads. To ask children merely to observe is pointless. They have to be directed to observe particular types of things. Again, the quality of worthwhileness of observations will depend upon the quality of the theories, of world views, which people bring to bear on their researches.

Freire discusses this under the heading of 'codification'. The process of abstraction depends upon, and creates, images, symbols, ideas, and concepts, that are, in one form or another, representations of concrete reality:

> Codification represents a given dimension of reality as individuals live it, and this dimension is proposed for their analysis in a context other than that in which they live.[9]

This procedure is vital to Freire's pedagogy and to his literacy programmes. In itself this is hierarchical. There are, and he quotes the American linguist Noam Chomsky on this, 'surface structures' and 'deep structures'. There are naive and sophisticated ways of representing phenomena; immediate and theoretical ways. In Freire's literacy programme, codification initially takes the form of a photograph or sketch which represents a real existent, or an existent constructed by the learners. The original words and descriptions used by the learners are gradually replaced by less immediate and more theoretical ones such as 'power', 'profit', and 'production'.

Freire maintains that an operation basic to the act of knowing is the gaining of distance from the knowable object. This is part of the reflective side of praxis. He opposes a total immersion in activity, on the grounds that it doesn't provide for the critical distancing in the act of knowing. We need to stand back and reflect upon our situation as an object of knowledge.[10] This is why peasants, immersed in a culture of silence, without the experience of being reflective and active subjects, face such an enormous epistemological obstacle. In western, urban situations, the pressures against distancing, or reflection, are as great. Where time is divided between travel, work, and rent, health and family worries, then opportunities for reflection are easily discounted.

Freire asserts that knowledge acquisition begins with problems, with puzzles, with tasks. Pedagogy must therefore be problematic:

> To be an act of knowing then, the adult literacy process must engage the learners in the constant problematising of their existential situations.[11]

Hence Freire poses to urban workers questions such as: 'Why is it that you can build high-rise office blocks and yet live in shanties?' Replies begin at the most basic level and gradually gain greater sophistication: poor soil, insects, lack of rain, transportation, marketing, imperialism. Freire is saying that learning will proceed better where it is based on problems that are relevant to the immediate situation, in other words where there is motivation to learn. This is why he castigates the use of readers which talk of 'Jack and Jill go up the hill'. Little wonder such programmes failed. Knowledge depends upon the uncovering of real problems and actual needs. Freire insists that the manner in which such knowledge is initially acquired cannot be dichotomised from the manner in which it is transmitted.

> If the development of scientific knowledge . . . cannot be separated from a problematic approach . . . neither can the apprehension of this knowledge.[12]

Freire contends that to know things is to know them in relation. To know a part is to know how it articulates within the whole. In Freire's process of codification, different impressions of the same object are elicited so the interrelations might be seen. Thus, the learners tend to replace a fragmented vision of reality with a total vision.[13] It is this total vision that we call knowledge. An analogy often used to portray this holist position is that of a group of blindfolded people around an elephant. One holds its tail and says he is holding a rope; another its leg and says he is holding a tree; another its trunk and says he is holding a snake. When the blindfolds are removed, they all see that they were holding different parts of the same whole. To understand a particular therefore is to see beyond it, to comprehend its wider underpinnings. For Freire, a critical consciousness sees facts in their casual and circumstantial interrelations. Naive and magical consciousness apprehends facts as they are in themselves, sometimes attributing to them a superior power. For example, at the immediate level a native in Brazil dies because he has pneumonia. On a more critical level however, he has pneumonia because he doesn't have food; he doesn't have food because he doesn't have money. This is important, because Brazil is no longer a subsistence economy, but a cash economy. He doesn't have money, not because he doesn't work, but because the international price of coffee has dropped, and this has occurred because of international economic factors. It is, of course, the latter understanding that Freire's pedagogy seeks to cultivate.

90

An important part of a holist approach to knowledge is, as Freire recognises, the historical dimension. Phenomena simply cannot be understood if they are viewed ahistorically. This is because an ahistorical understanding tends to see situations and social realities as necessary, or immutable, when they are actually contingent and changeable. Thus ahistoricism is conducive to ideological misunderstanding. Naive consciousness does not just see particulars, but particulars without history. Ideological institutions can sanctify contingent circumstances and give them the appearance of permanent realities.

One of the more perplexing areas of Freire's epistemology may be designated as 'fallibilism'. Others might refer to it as 'relativism', or 'subjectivism', or 'scepticism'. Freire's fallibilism is contained in statements like the following:

> Further, critical consciousness always submits that caus-ality to analysis; what is true today may not be so tomorrow. Naive consciousness sees causality as a static, established fact, and thus is deceived in its perception.[14]

At the very least, Freire is asserting here that no knowledge is ever complete. This is not particularly controversial, as many would agree that we see through a glass darkly. The term 'fallible' indicates just this – that our ideas can be improved upon, and our understandings deepened. But to say that knowledge is never complete is not to say that what is true today may be false tomorrow. If this is unqualified, then it must be a form of scepticism. Freire does have a developmentalist, dialectical, and dynamic view of reality: in other words, a process ontology. If reality is changing, if it is in flux, if we never step into the same river twice as Heracleitus said, then our knowledge may become outdated. In this sense, what was true may now be false, but the property of 'truth' no longer applies to the same reality-statement couple because reality has changed. This is a com-monplace. However, Freire's process ontology, coupled with a fallibilist epistemology, is a powerful aid to tolerance, and an inhibitor of dogmatism. There is enough in Freire to indicate that he is not a relativist. One idea is not as good as another. Various features of his theory – the naive versus critical consciousness distinction; the very culture-circle movement itself – all suggest this. Similarly, he is not a sceptic. Knowledge is possible, otherwise why the pedagogy, why the scholarship and analysis, why the hope?

This account of Freire's epistemology has emphasised the point that the purpose of knowledge is action. We know in order to do. Freire is unambiguous in his rejection of the idea that knowledge exists for its own sake.[15] For Freire, humanity is incomplete, and the world is likewise incomplete. Our ontological vocation is to humanise ourselves by transforming the oppressive structures of our world. The exercise of human intellect is tied into this vocation: we reason in order to transform. Moreover, people exist in societies which have a history, and this history is one of power struggles and class struggles. Freire points out that to do nothing in such situations is to do something. For to do nothing is to support the exploitation of the powerless by the powerful. Thus people must act. Marx and Freire see this action as intimately connected with intellectual development. For them people are cognitive, emotional and active, in a unity which they describe as praxis. Interpretation cannot occur without action. It is even more incomprehensible that, given interpretation, action should not follow. That many people in capitalist societies have difficulty with this is a clear reflection of the anti-human culture which we have developed. And this, in turn, is a reflection of the fundamental rupture in the productive base of our society. The features of Freire's theory of knowledge highlighted here have implications for all aspects of educational endeavour. Above all, Freire demonstrates that the content and methods of education are not neutral, but essentially political in their nature.

7. Contributions to the Thought of Paulo Freire
by Robert Mackie

I began, as a man of the third world, to elaborate not a mechanical method for adult literacy learning, but an educational theory generated in the womb of the culture of silence itself – a theory which could become in practice not the voice of the culture, but one of the instruments of that still faltering voice. *Paulo Freire*

The educational theory of Paulo Freire has many roots. It has evolved, developed and matured against the background of an extensive, continuing personal commitment and intellectual eclecticism. Understanding Freire not only requires us to unravel the complex fabric of his thought, but also to detect its origins, traditions and disparate borrowings. The questions, where do Freire's ideas come from, and how do they fit into the broader framework of contemporary social, political and educational thought, are the two underlying concerns of this chapter. Answers to such questions should go some way towards dispelling the widespread, and misleading impression that Freire's writing is dense, opaque and impenetrable – comprehensible and relevant only to Brazilians. The following pages are an attempt to sketch in Freire's intellectual roots and context, while critical exploration of internal tensions and evaluation of the overall coherence of his theory will be confined to brief comments, principally bearing upon his politics. A more rigorous and systematic appraisal along these lines is begun in the following chapter. Here however, the overriding intention is to make Freire's origins clear.

Components of Paulo Freire's Theory

(i) Early Liberalism

Any search for the sources of Freire's ideas must begin with

93

his own practice, particularly his work in north-east Brazil during the two decades immediately following the second world war. Earlier chapters of this book have dealt with the social, political, economic and educational milieu in which Freire's theory was conceived. Yet it must be stressed that his activities in Recife concerning adult literacy remain as substantial and significant factors in his development. Equally important, however, is the recognition that politically he has moved far beyond the liberal, democratic stance which informs his early book, *Education: the Practice of Freedom*, (1967).

During those post-war years Freire conceived of Brazil as a society in transition. Where formerly it had been closed and silent now, under the impact of technological development and comparatively more liberal government Brazil was gradually opening. It was experiencing a new sense of national cohesion and identity. Freire, in the 1950s and early 1960s, embraced and supported moves by Brazilian intellectuals to establish an authentic national culture. *Education: the Practice of Freedom,* and indeed all of Freire's works, contain regular references to Brazilian sociologists, economists and historians, especially Francisco Weffort, Gilberto Freyre, Fernando de Azeveda and Alvara Vieira Pinto. Moreover, the formation of the *Instituto Superior de Estudos Brasilieros* (ISEB) in Juscelino Kubitschek's presidency proved to be, as Freire says, an experiment of the greatest importance in graduate and university instruction. The ISEB intellectuals took Brazilian reality as their project, seeking to identify themselves with the country as it really was rather than continuing to perceive it through European eyes. Freire comments that two important consequences followed this development:

> the creative power of intellectuals who placed themselves at the service of the national culture, and commitment to the destiny of the reality those intellectuals considered and assumed as their own.[1]

Viewed from this perspective Freire's work in literacy can be seen as wholly consonant with the emerging Brazilian national consciousness. It is in this context also that Freire laments the years previously wasted by his compatriots who, in search of prefabri-

94

cated solutions, turned to societies they considered superior to their own.[2]

Supplementing this earnest avowal of Brazilian nationalism is considerable evidence of the influence of European and North American liberalism. *Education: the Practice of Freedom* is peppered with favourable references to Seymour Lipset, John Dewey, Karl Popper, Alfred Whitehead, and Karl Mannheim. This provides a clear indication that the intellectual framework employed by Freire in delineating Brazilian moves towards democracy owed as much to overseas writing as it did to indigenous scholarship. Further, it demonstrates one important and abiding feature of Freire's intellect: its cosmopolitan roots and willingness to synthesise varied and diverse influences. His capacity in this regard is one factor among several that enables him to be cleared from charges of narrow parochialism.

It is from Karl Popper specifically that Freire gleans his notion of Brazil as a society in the process of opening.[3] In this transitional phase education plays a crucial role, not simply in terms of teaching literacy, but as a form of

> cultural action by means of which the Brazilian people could learn, in place of the old passivity, new attitudes and habits of participation and intervention.[4]

While recognising the potential force of education in this regard, Freire is also mindful of its limitations. Education is not a 'miraculous process capable by itself of effecting the changes necessary to move a nation from one epoch to another'.[5] Rather it was just one of many means by which Brazilians were to learn social and political responsibility.

At the time when he was the co-ordinator of the Adult Education Project directed from Recife University, Freire was a political liberal and democrat. Demonstrating an indebtedness to both Dewey and Mannheim, Freire writes that the Brazilian people,

> could be helped to learn democracy through the exercise of democracy; for that knowledge, above all others, can only be assimilated experimentally . . . democracy and democratic education are founded on faith in people, on

95

the belief that they not only can but should discuss the problems of their country, of their continent, their world, their work, the problems of democracy itself.[6]

In words strongly reminiscent of Dewey, Freire contends that 'before it becomes a political term, democracy is a form of life'.[7] Freire endorses Mannheim's argument that as democratic processes become more widespread, it is difficult and undesirable to allow the masses to stay in ignorance.[8] Thus the educational programme Freire implemented was designed to produce critical consciousness, or *conscientizacao*, so adults could actively participate in the emerging forms of democratic life. In rejecting attempts at 'massification' through formal schooling, and by launching culture circles Freire sought vitality in education as distinct from the transmission of what Whitehead has called 'inert ideas'.[9] Freire argues that by deliberately placing adult illiterates in critical confrontation with their problems, they can be made agents of their own recuperation. In this process, especially if the initial pitfalls of fanaticism and irrationality are to be avoided, education must develop, in the illiterate, *conscientizacao*. Freire delineates this in almost classic liberal terms as

> depth in the interpretation of problems; by the substitution of causal principles for magical explanations; by the testing of one's own 'findings' and openness to revision . . . by refusing to transfer responsibility; by rejecting passive positions; by soundness of argumentation; by the practice of dialogue rather than polemics . . . by accepting what is valid in both old and new.[10]

Critical consciousness, Freire concludes, is characteristic of authentically democratic regimes. It corresponds to highly permeable, interrogative, restless and dialogical forms of life.[11] While later discussion of conscientisation is couched in dialectical and revolutionary terms, Freire's analysis of it in *Education: the Practice of Freedom* is located firmly within a liberal, democratic framework. In fact, this volume closes with an affirmation of Mannheim's notion of 'militant democracy'. This is

> a democracy which does not fear the people, which

suppresses privilege, which can plan without becoming rigid which defends itself without hate, which is nourished by a critical spirit rather than irrationality.[12]

The same tone is evident at this time in Freire's brief treatment of radicalism. In the transitional society of Brazil he comments, the deepening clash between old and new encouraged an emotional climate where choices became more clear cut. Within this context radicalisation involved:

> increased commitment to the position one has chosen. It is predominantly critical, loving, humble and communicative, and therefore a positive stance. The person who has made a radical option does not deny another's right to choose, nor try to impose his or her own choice . . . he or she tries to convince and convert, not to crush the opponent. The radical does, however, have the duty, imposed by love itself, to react against the violence of those who try to silence him or her – of those who, in the name of freedom, kill his or freedom and their own.[13]

Radicalism, for Freire, is clearly differentiated from sectarianism whether of the right or left. The sectarian not only disrespects the choices of others but regards him- or herself as the proprietor of history, manoeuvering the people into support of pre-ordained goals. Sectarianism is thus arrogant, emotional, and uncritical.[14]

(ii) Modern Theology and Catholic Radicalism

To fully grasp Freire's position on both *conscientizacao* and radicalism two additional factors are important: the impact key theologians made on his thinking; and the Brazilian phenomenon of grassroots catholic political and cultural movements for social change. Taken together these influences enable us to recognise that Freire's espousal of radical critical consciousness was widely shared among Brazil's confraternity. Moreover, his statements on God, faith and the church are clear and vigorous expressions of the need for social engagement and radical action by those who profess to be christians. For example, when castigating the neutral posture of the church in the face of social injustice, Freire writes:

washing one's hands of the conflict between the powerful and the powerless means to side with the powerful, not to be neutral.[15]

Similarly, his reading of the gospel leads him to declare,

> I never find anything in the gospel to tell me to be a reactionary. I can't reconcile christian love with the exploitation of human beings. God is an invitation to me to make history. God is thus a presence in history; he is not my boss but my friend.[16]

To many christians, and especially catholics, Freire's views would seem highly unorthodox and controversial. Yet it must be stressed that he has always held deep and strong christian beliefs which are continually expressed, not in the form of quietistic piety but as a compassionate, active and wholehearted struggle for the liberation of humanity on earth. It is the purpose of this section to explain the intellectual roots of this contribution to Freire's thought, and briefly indicate the practical form his emerging radicalism took.

In 1961 and 1963 Pope John XXIII published two encyclicals, *Mater et Magistra* and *Pacem in Terris*, both of which had profound consequences for the catholic world, particularly those living in poverty and oppression in South America. *Mater et Magistra* gave prominence to the idea of 'socialisation' which was defined as 'the progressive multiplication of relations in society, with different forms of life and activity, and juridical institutionalisation'.[17] This marked a distinct shift from the previously pejorative sense of 'socialisation' as marking the encroachment of the state on the private lives of citizens. Pope John went on to declare that 'socialisation' was

> the fruit and expression of a natural tendency, almost irrepressible, in human beings – the tendency to join together to attain objectives which are beyond the capacity and means at the disposal of single individuals.[18]

The effect of this pronouncement was to sanction the activities of those who struggled together in pursuit of goals which were beyond them individually. In the context of Brazil at this time, and in Freire's thought especially, the papal encyclicals gave a strong fillip to the exposure of myths formerly considered indispensable for the preservation of the status quo. In *Pedagogy of the Oppressed* (1970), Freire inveighs against those national and international elites who foster the myth of charity by the performance of selective 'good deeds'. Drawing on *Mater et Magistra* for support, Freire condemns

> the myth that the dominant elites, 'recognising their duties', promote the advancement of the people, so that the people in a gesture of gratitude, should accept the words of the elites and conform to them.[19]

When *Pacem in Terris* was published in April 1963, the central national committee of Brazilian bishops released an accompanying declaration. This spoke of the profound aspirations of the people who do not participate in the Brazilian process. Later it referred to the minority, possessing the means and finding all doors open to them, while the majority were deprived of the fundamental and natural rights enunciated in the papal encyclical.[20] It is principally against a background of these documents and the theological contributions of Teilhard de Chardin, Henrique de Lima Pe Vaz, Emanuel Mounier and Reinhold Niebuhr that Freire clarified his thinking on religion, the church and education.

Although recognition of Teilhard's contribution to catholic theology did not come until after his death in 1955, he has since then emerged as a major influence in the catholic world. His studies in palaeontology prompted an early and abiding interest in evolutionary theory, leading him to propose in *The Phenomenon of Man* (1961) a unified and integrated view of the universe. Teilhard conceived of 'socialisation' as a process of growth among humanity which was the result of an ultimately inevitable and irreversible dynamic grounded in the biological and psychosocial nature of human beings. Teilhard stressed our final 'hominisation' as we collectively evolve towards the 'point omega', which is a finality of perfect evolution. 'Point omega' is conceived as the Man-God whose second coming will bring about the plentitude of the universe of persons.[21]

From the standpoint of Henrique Pe Vaz, historical

consciousness depends upon a critical and intentional reflection on the historical process itself. The present is understood as both a result of the past, and as potentiality for the future. For Vaz when we look critically at our world, we become aware of the fact that by our actions we can transform it. It is transformation by people themselves which not only humanises the world, but is also the specific obligation of modern christianity. Vaz argues that refusal to shoulder this destiny of creation, or to appropriate it into egotism, is original sin and the fount of all evil.[22]

For Paulo Freire the formulations of Teilhard and Vaz are crucial. Their concepts of socialisation and humanisation underly Freire's notions of humanity, human relationships, consciousness, praxis and conscientisation. When Freire writes of people as beings in and with the world, he stresses Teilhard's point that we are consciously reflective towards both ourselves and the world we inhabit. Quoting Teilhard, Freire says people are not only beings who know, but beings who know they know.[23] Or again, this time echoing Vaz, Freire contends 'consciousness of and action upon reality are therefore inseparable constituents of the transforming act by which people become beings of relation'.[24] Moreover, conscientisation is possible only because human consciousness, although conditioned, can recognise itself as such. Because our reflective presence impregnates the world, only we can humanise or dehumanise. And since this reflectiveness is not possible without history and a physical context, there is no here relative to a there which is not connected to a now, a before, and an after. 'Not only do people make history', Freire concludes,

> but they can recount the history of this mutual making. In becoming 'hominised', as Teilhard de Chardin puts it, in the process of evolution, people become capable of having a biography.[25]

The impact of modern theology on Freire is further amplified through the contributions of Emanuel Mounier and Reinhold Niebuhr. In the early 1960s the writing of Mounier and especially his journal *Esprit* became known to Brazilian catholics in Portuguese translations. Mounier, working within a christian existentialist framework, focused on persons rather than institutions; on the goal of changing human nature, rather than the institutional context in which such change might take place. While affirming continually his faith in socialism, as a corporately organised and decentralised social order, Mounier also expressed a revolutionary romanticism: 'Our fundamental belief is that a revolution is an affair of people, that its principal efficacy is the internal flame which is communicated from person to person, when people offer themselves gratuitously to one another.'[26]

A further aspect of Mounier's thought is pertinent for Freire. Along with other existentialists Mounier is concerned with 'authenticity', which is attained by honest, considered and careful choices. Through such choices a person becomes edified; we have no other essence apart from our existence. This emphasis on authenticity underpinned the horror many catholic radicals, including Freire, felt towards any attempt at curtailing the freedom of choice of the people. Although catholic radicals were conscious of the need to organise the masses, this was only to come after they had become aware of the problems involved and opted for change. The manipulation, or 'massification', of the people by their leaders was to be resolutely opposed.[27] The impact of Mounier's work on Freire can be seen most clearly in the latter's emphasis on continual, authentic dialogue between revolutionary leaders and the people. Dialogue facilitates human communication by which people become 'available' to one another.[28] To impede such communication is to deny our authenticity and reduce us to the status of 'things' – a job, Freire says, for oppressors, not revolutionaries.[29]

Complementing Mounier's influence is the writing of American protestant theologian Reinhold Niebuhr, particularly his *Moral Man and Immoral Society* (1932). This alerted Freire both to the reality of classes in society, and to the conservative nature of paternalistic moralism. Thus, when discussing the reaction of dominant elites to the emergence of the oppressed, Freire, following Niebuhr, asserts that the elites can condemn the violence of a strike by workers and in the same breath call upon the state to use violence in putting it down.[30] Oppressors never see themselves as violent. A similar tone and indebtedness, are evident where Freire talks of those who see in *conscientizacao* some kind of magical tool, or idealistic 'third way' that will create mutual understanding, peace and harmony. At bottom such idealistic visions only serve the oppressors, since they fail to recognise that when collective power exploits weakness it can never be dislodged unless power is raised against it. Such mythologising of *conscientizacao* is an obstacle to the process of liberation because, in emptying the term of its dialectical content, it appears as a panacea and the gap between class consciousness and consciousness of class needs is obscured.[31]

Niebuhr's influence also lies behind Freire's disenchantment with 'catholic action'. This movement, founded by Jacques Maritain and widespread in South America, urged christians to be active in the world on behalf of democracy and social justice. Politically its stance was ameliorative, consensual and liberal. Freire and his wife Elza joined the movement soon after the second world war. Together they worked among well-to-do couples in comfortable homes in Recife, trying to change their hearts and develop the contradiction between social privilege and the radical demands of christian faith. As Freire later reflected,

> we were very naive, because to change hearts without changing structures which prevent good hearts is insane. When we say we are defending christian faith we are often defending our class interests.[32]

Gradually the reactionary nature of these activities became clear to him, and Freire left the movement to concentrate on the problem of adult illiteracy among Brazil's urban and rural poor. It has already been made clear how this work drew heavily on the notion of *conscientizacao*. What, perhaps, is not so well recognised is that *conscientizacao*, far from being a term located in Freire's writings, enjoyed wide and popular currency among radical catholics before, during, and after, his work on literacy.[33]

Emanuel de Kadt, in his study of *Catholic Radicals in Brazil* (1970) points out:

> no exploited or downtrodden people is able to take its destiny into its own hands until after it has become aware of its situation in the world. Such awareness constitutes the

102

basis for action. Hence the importance which Brazil's radical catholics attached to *conscientizacao*.[34]

In addition to programmes of mass literacy, *conscientizacao* was prompted by more general movements of popular culture. Four years before the coup of April 1964 the socialist mayor of Recife, Miguel Arraes, sponsored one such movement that incorporated Freire's literacy method. Within two years several other states had formed organisations financed by public funds that tried to reach and stir the masses by means of plays, films and leaflets, all of which focused on socio-political problems. The intention of such endeavours was to foster the integration of all Brazilians in the struggle for economic, political and cultural liberation. After April 1964 however, enthusiasm for these movements of national emancipation abruptly ceased.[35]

Yet in many ways the brief flourishing of *cultura popular* expresses a central dimension of the political stance taken by catholic radicals in Brazil: namely, its profoundly humanist orientation. One group, for instance, stated its obligations in terms that could equally describe Freire's own concerns:

> Our only obligation is towards human beings. Towards the Brazilian people first and foremost . . . [they] who grow up stupid and illiterate, outcasts from the blessings of culture, of creative opportunities, and of truly human roads to real freedom; who die a beast's anonymous death, cast down on the hard ground of their misery. Thus we struggle for human beings with human beings. Our struggle is the struggle of all.[36]

The tenor of this, and other similar humanist declarations, owed much to the post-stalinist disenchantment many radicals, socialists and neo-marxists felt with the results of the Russian revolution. Freire certainly endorses such sentiments:

> the moment the new regime hardens into a dominating 'bureaucracy' the humanist dimension of the struggle is lost and it is no longer possible to speak of liberation. This rigidity . . . refers to the revolution which becomes stagnant and turns against the people, using the old repressive, bureaucratic state apparatus.[37]

103

For Freire, as for many others, socialist humanism was seen as a form of politics preferable to that practised by the Brazilian Communist Party. The widely felt distrust of that party derived from what was perceived to be its advocacy of piecemeal economic improvements, and its collaboration with the national bourgeoisie. In short, it lacked a truly revolutionary perspective. Consequently late in 1962, when communist party members became influential in Recife, Freire transferred his literacy programme from the aegis of the municipality to the Cultural Extension Service of Recife University.[38] That Freire should make such a move was entirely consistent with the general political stance of catholic radicals at this time.

(iii) Revolutionary Socialism

Since Paulo Freire has continually asserted the non-neutrality of education and repeatedly stressed its essentially political nature, the question of his own politics becomes central to any understanding of his work. It can scarcely be denied that Freire is vitally concerned with alienation, liberation, praxis and revolution. Indeed such concerns have become paramount in his writing during the years of his exile. *Pedagogy of the Oppressed* and *Cultural Action for Freedom* (1970) expresses a political position sharply to the left of that found in *Education: the Practice of Freedom* (1967). Freire has put much of his liberal democratic politics far behind and today he is decidedly more radical. The reasons for this shift are both personal and intellectual. The very fact that Joao Goulart's mildly reformist government was brutally overthrown, and an authoritarian military regime installed in power, dealt a severe blow to Freire's notions of militant democracy. In his search for an explanation of this tragedy, Freire turned increasingly to the writings of Marx, and began to study more closely the activities of revolutionary leaders like Fidel Castro, Ernesto 'Che' Guevara, Mao Tse-tung, and Amilcar Cabral. The result of this inquiry is that in terms of broad political positions – conservative, liberal, socialist – Freire today would be firmly in the socialist camp.

Yet there are many diverse political philosophies that can be, and are, subsumed under the general heading of 'socialism'. The question, on closer analysis, really comes down to deciding

104

what kind of socialism Freire espouses. Speaking generally, there are three possible answers to that question: humanist socialism; revolutionary socialism; and marxist socialism, or communism.

Adherents to the first of these positions, for example Erich Fromm, and the younger Leszek Kolakowski, believe in the ideal of human unity and profess an optimistic faith in the future of humanity. They maintain a view of Marx which emphasises alienation, and assert that the social and economic relations of capitalism distort and disfigure the possibilities for full development of individuality. As humanists these socialists concentrate on human nature, and the unfolding of human potential. As socialists these humanists tend to deny the economic bases of social and political structures, playing down the possibility of violent revolution as a means of social transformation. Similarly, the primacy of class struggle in Marx's thought is often excluded in favour of a more idealised stress on human potency.[39]

While it is clear that there are many elements of humanist socialism in Freire's politics, it is equally apparent that he goes further than this and adopts a more ostensibly revolutionary stand. A pronounced characteristic of Freire's political and educational theory is the support he gives to charismatic revolutionary leaders. Indeed the pedagogical function of the revolutionary process is heavily stressed. Moreover, in his open discussion of class struggle and violence Freire demarcates himself from the timorous, idealised appeals to human solidarity that typify socialist humanism. By recognising that the dialectical relationship between opposing classes can only be resolved through the struggle of the oppressed for their liberation, Freire endorses revolution as the central component of his pedagogy of the oppressed. If Niebuhr has made Freire aware of social classes, then Marx has crystallised this as class struggle. So in suggesting Freire be considered a revolutionary socialist recognition is paid to his emphasis on both the humanistic bases of revolution and its roots in collective praxis.

Why then is Freire not a marxist socialist, or a communist? Several reasons are pertinent in this regard. Firstly, Marx's theory embraces a great deal more than class struggle. It is fundamental to Marx that the economic and material bases of society determine its social and political arrangements. That is to

105

say, any adequate analysis of society must be grounded in an understanding of the forces and relations of production. Marxist accounts of revolutionary praxis emphasise this as both the outcome of economic contradictions inherent in capitalism, and as the solution to them. Hence the primacy in Marx of economic and historical materialism as the bases for revolution. This emphasis is not echoed in Freire. One consequence of such an omission, as Marx and Engels recognised, is that talk of revolution then tends to become utopian and idealised.

This highlights a second reason why Freire cannot be regarded as a marxist socialist. For Marx revolution is conceived in political and economic terms since it is transformation here that provides the foundations of a socialist society. Freire, however, ignores the political economy of revolution in favour of an emphasis on its cultural dimension:

> Revolution is always cultural, whether it be in the phase of denouncing an oppressive society and proclaiming the advent of a just society, or in the phase of the new society inaugurated by the revolution. In the new society the revolutionary process becomes cultural revolution.[40]

Formulating a conception of revolution in these terms allows Freire ample scope to signify its pedagogical character. Yet at the same time it obscures the fundamental issues of economic and political power. It is significant in this connection that Freire's own work in Brazil and Guinea-Bissau depended upon the prior political success of Joao Goulart and Amilcar Cabral.

Finally, Freire could not be seen as a communist, in the sense of party membership or affiliation, and this for a reason already mentioned. His suspicion of Brazilian communists working in his literacy programme led him to transfer it from Recife municipality to the university. Warranted or not, Freire's misgivings about communists stand as a common reaction to the political exigencies of the cold war and stalinism. Both his theoretical writing and practical involvement lend support to movements of national liberation in formerly colonised territories. This aspect of his work could indeed be viewed as a more radical expression of an earlier liberal nationalism.

106

It is suggested, then, that Paulo Freire's politics are most correctly conceived in terms of a revolutionary socialism. This has its initial roots in humanism and nationalism, but is radically transformed by his adoption of some aspects of Marx, espousal of revolution and violence, along with a clear recognition of the need for revolutionary leadership. The following discussion attempts to trace the sources of Freire's revolutionary socialism.

The framework for Freire's analysis of oppression and liberation is established largely by reference to the writing of Erich Fromm, Albert Memmi, and to a lesser extent Frantz Fanon. The ideas contained in Fromm's *Fear of Freedom* (1942), *Marx's Concept of Man* (1961), *Socialist Humanism* (1965) and *The Heart of Man* (1966) all find a ready acceptance in Freire. At the outset of *Pedagogy of the Oppressed* Freire makes his standpoint quite explicit. The education he is concerned with has, as its great humanistic and historical task, the liberation of both oppressor and oppressed. In fact, it would be a contradiction in terms if the former not only defended, but actually implemented a liberating education.[41] Yet there are considerable difficulties confronting the oppressed and preventing them from fulfilling this task. Principal among these is the identification of the oppressed with their masters. All too often the oppressed seek to become oppressors in their turn. In explaining this situation Freire follows Fromm directly and contends that the oppressed are fearful of freedom since they have internalised and adopted the image of the oppressor. Alienated and divided within their innermost being, the oppressed fear freedom. If they are to struggle for liberation then images implanted by the oppressor must be rejected. Freire suggests this can be done through a critical confrontation with, and transformation of, their social reality. Freedom, he affirms, is not an ideal or a myth but rather an indispensable condition of the quest for human completion.[42]

In delineating the social psychology of oppression Freire emphasises the lust for direct, material, concrete possession of the world and the people without which the oppressor consciousness could not even exist. Oppressors do not see that in the egoistic pursuit of having, they suffocate in their possessions and no longer are: they merely have. Everything surrounding such a consciousness is reduced to an object of domination. People and material objects become merely inanimate things. Drawing upon Fromm directly, Freire highlights the sadistic nature of oppression:

> the pleasure in complete domination over another person is the very essence of the sadistic drive . . . since by complete and absolute control the living loses one essential quality of life – freedom.[43]

In educational terms this necrophilic consciousness finds its analogue in the banking concept. This form of mechanistic education attempts, by controlling thought and action, to adjust students to the world rather than developing their capacities to transform it. Such an education, Freire declares, serves the interests of oppression. It is nourished by the worship of death, not life.[44]

Supplementing Freire's indebtedness to Fromm are insights contained in Albert Memmi's *The Coloniser and the Colonised* (1957), and Frantz Fanon's *The Wretched of the Earth* (1961). It is indicative of the shift in Freire's thinking that, whereas Memmi and Fanon figure prominently in his analysis of oppression and liberation, they are absent from the two essays comprising *Education: the Practice of Freedom*. In depicting the psychology of oppression Freire, by utilising the insights of Memmi and Fanon into colonial dependence in Algeria, is able to amplify and clarify the mentality which produced the 'third world'. Freire's work emphatically echoes Memmi's declaration:

> I am unconditionally opposed to all forms of oppression. For me oppression is the greatest calamity of humanity. It diverts and pollutes the best energies of humanity – of oppressed and oppressor alike. For if colonisation destroys the colonised, it also rots the coloniser.[45]

Freire's analysis finds further support in Memmi's contention that where the ideology of a governing class is given adherence by the governed, then the dominated practically confirm the roles assigned to them. Such a situation disfigures both oppressor and oppressed: the former worry only about privileges and their defence; the latter acquiesce and compromise in their defeat.[46]

The essential dilemma facing the oppressed is, in Memmi's words, that 'It is not easy to escape mentally from a concrete situation to refuse its ideology, while continuing to live with its actual relationships.'[47] In short, the pedagogy of the oppressed can be seen as a struggle against the colonisation of man's mental territory. For both Memmi and Freire liberation can only come through revolution. 'The refusal of the colonised', Memmi writes,

> cannot be anything but absolute, that is, not only revolt, but a revolution . . . to live the colonised needs to do away with colonisation. To become a human being we must do away with the colonised being that we have become.[48]

If humanist concerns for liberation are the principal legacies that Fromm and Memmi bequeath to Freire, then confronting revolution as a political solution brings him directly to Marx. Freire argues that people do not exist apart from the world, but in constant interaction with it. Social reality is produced and transformed by human activity. Just as Marx affirmed that people change circumstances, so Freire locates the roots of his pedagogy in the need for critical intervention by the oppressed in their reality. One of the essential tools for achieving such critical intervention is language, since this shapes consciousness. Both Marx and Freire agree that language is as old as consciousness. In fact, language is consciousness in practice. Since they arise from the necessity of intercourse with others, both language and consciousness are social products, and remain so as long as people exist.[49] Consequently, Freire's approach to literacy involves more than the psychological and mechanical domination of techniques for reading and writing. Rather 'it is to dominate these techniques in terms of consciousness . . . a self-transformation producing a stance of intervention in one's context'.[50]

However, by acting on the world and changing it, people at the same time change their own nature. In highlighting this point Marx is emphasising the dynamism of human development, where people, through their actions, literally make themselves. Consciousness and activity are, for Marx and Freire, a unity conceived in terms of revolutionary praxis. Freire expresses it as action and reflection upon the world in order to transform it. Activism or verbalism in isolation from each other are insufficient: authentic praxis, and hence liberation, requires the continual synthesis of critical reflection with action.[51]

Freire fully understands that the revolutionary praxis he is advocating will take place in a context of class antagonism and conflict. 'In a class society,' he says, 'the power elite necessarily determines what education will be, and therefore its objectives.' He adds,

> it would be supremely naive to imagine that the elite would in any way promote or accept an education which stimulated the oppressed to discover the raison d'etre of the social structure. The most that could be expected is that the elite might permit talk of such education, and occasional experiments which could be immediately suppressed should the status quo be threatened.[52]

In stating what is probably the major obstacle to revolutionary praxis, Freire clearly endorses Marx's contention that the dominant ideas of every epoch are necessarily those of the ruling class. The ideological hegemony of the ruling class is established, as Freire makes abundantly plain, through strategies of conquest, divide and rule, manipulation, and cultural invasion. So when he warns that liberation is not a call to armchair revolution, but of necessity involves the transformation of concrete situations which beget oppression, Freire means the disappearance of oppressors as a dominant class.[53] In effect, revolutionary praxis not only challenges the intervention of ruling elites in education, but seeks as well to rescue it from their influences.

Central to this struggle, and to Freire's politics, is the role assigned to revolutionary leaders. Those who commit themselves to the people must undergo a profound rebirth that is so radical as not to allow of ambiguous behaviour. For Freire this takes the form of an 'easter' experience, where the leaders 'die as elitists so as to be resurrected on the side of the oppressed, that they be born again with the beings who were not allowed to be'.[54] To successfully undergo this rebirth requires a renunciation of the myths of oppression, namely:

110

the myth of their 'superiority', of their purity of soul, of their virtues, their wisdom, the myth that they 'save the poor', the myth of the neutrality of the church, theology, education, science, technology, the myth of their own impartiality.[55]

Such an experience, Freire asserts, results in a profound change in one's intentions towards the world, that is, in consciousness. This does not occur by lectures, sermons, or seminars 'but by the actions of human beings in the world'.[56]

Revolutionary leaders, having made their easter, will engage in political action on the side of the oppressed. Superficial conversions, which lack trust in the oppressed and their ability to reason, carry twin dangers: that of falling into slogans, communiques or monologues; or of exploiting the emotional dependence of the oppressed. The correct method of revolutionary leadership, Freire suggests, lies in dialogue. 'The conviction of the oppressed that they must fight for their liberation is not,' he affirms, 'a gift bestowed by the revolutionary leadership, but the result of their own *conscientizacao*.'[57]

Freire is convinced that in the revolutionary movement there can be no dichotomy between leaders and the people. 'Revolutionary praxis is a unity,' he writes, 'and the leaders cannot treat the oppressed as their possession'.[58] Dialogue between the leaders and the people is radically necessary to every authentic revolution. There is not one stage for dialogue and another for revolution. On the contrary, dialogue is the essence of revolutionary action. Moreover, it is this line of argument which leads Freire to assert that the revolutionary process is eminently pedagogical, since it involves openness and communion, not imperviousness and mistrust.[59]

If revolutionary leaders are crucial to the struggle for liberation, then who, in history, comes nearest to embodying the qualities Freire seeks? When discussing individual personalities in this context Freire most often mentions Mao Tse-tung, Fidel Castro, Che Guevara, Camillo Torres, and Amilcar Cabral. The general tenor of his argument suggests the conclusion that these five men are exemplary revolutionary leaders. Mao-Tse-tung's remark, 'We must teach the masses clearly what we have received from them confusedly', is seen by Freire to contain an entire dialogical theory. This is elaborated more fully in Mao's contention that all work done for the masses must start from their needs and not from the desire of any well-intentioned individual.[60] Fidel Castro is similarly praised for identifying with the people who endured the brutal violence of Batista's dictatorship. Freire claims this 'required bravery on the part of the leaders to love the people sufficiently to be willing to sacrifice themselves for them . . . so it was that Fidel never entered into contradiction with the people'.[61]

Freire reserves for Che Guevara the highest accolade of revolutionary leadership. Of him Freire writes:

> Che Guevara is an example of the unceasing witness revolutionary leadership gives to dialogue with the people. The more we study his work, the more we perceive his conviction that anyone who wants to become a true revolutionary must be in 'communion' with the people. Guevara did not hesitate to recognise the capacity to love as an indispensable condition for authentic revolutionaries.[62]

Revolution, then, is not irreconcilable with love. Even the distortion capitalism imposes on the word 'love' cannot prevent the revolution being essentially loving in character, nor can it prevent revolutionaries affirming their love of life.[63]

In terms of their contribution to Freire's political stance, Mao, Castro, Guevara and the others can be seen as symbolic of the leadership he desires. Freire conceives their action as revolutionaries primarily in cultural terms, with the political nature of their activities continually implied. With its clear statement of class struggle and revolutionary leadership, Freire's political position can be seen to have shifted away from liberal nationalism and become decidedly more radical. However, if as he suggests the concrete structures of an oppressive reality are to be transformed, then a more specifically materialist analysis of revolutionary situations is required than he provides. There is more than a tendency for him to idealise and romanticise revolutionary leaders who 'make their easter' or 'bear unceasing witness' to the struggle. The politics Freire advocates would be better served by dissolving, rather than augmenting, the legends surrounding Mao, Fidel and Che.

This point gains further pertinence when consideration is given to the presence of violence in revolutionary change. It is to Freire's credit that he does not opt for a pacifist resolution of the oppressor-oppressed contradiction. In a situation of class struggle dialogue is impossible between antagonists.[64] This is because dialogue can only occur in a context of love, humility, faith and critical consciousness – qualities that are absent in the oppressor and stunted in the oppressed. Consequently, Freire is perfectly consistent, and not arbitrarily dogmatic, when he writes:

> once a popular revolution has come to power, the fact that the new power has the ethical duty to repress any attempt to restore the old oppressive power by no means signifies that the revolution is contradicting its dialogical character.[65]

'Dialogue,' Freire concludes, 'between the former oppressors and the oppressed as antagonistic classes was not possible before the revolution: it continues to be impossible afterward.'[66] By recognising violence as a factor in revolution Freire is not deserting his christian, specifically catholic, faith. Catholics have long recognised that violent rebellion is justified provided: the cause is just; that there is reasonable hope of success; that peaceful means have shown themselves to be ineffective; and that the means chosen are themselves just.[67] As Freire remarks, 'there would be no oppressed had there been no prior situation of violence to establish their subjugation.'[68] It is those who oppress that initiate violence, those who despise that initiate hatred. Force is used by the strong who have emasculated the weak.

However, Freire also asserts that acts of violent rebellion can initiate love. This apparently paradoxical situation is explained as follows:

> as the oppressors dehumanise others and violate their rights, they themselves also become dehumanised. As the oppressed, fighting to be human, take away the oppressor's power to dominate and suppress, they restore to the

113

oppressors the humanity they had lost in the exercise of oppression.[69]

The point Freire makes is that violence by the oppressed is motivated by love, not hatred. Just as the very raison d'etre of oppression precludes dialogue with oppressors as a means towards liberation, so also does it make violence an inevitable and integral part of revolutionary change. This conclusion further indicates how far Freire has travelled from his earlier advocacy of militant democracy. That he is fully aware of this shift in his position can be demonstrated from remarks made during a World Council of Churches seminar in September 1974. Reflecting upon his previous naive and liberal view of conscientisation, Freire comments:

> My mistake was not that I recognised the fundamental importance of a knowledge of reality in the process of its change, but rather, that I did not take these two different moments – the knowledge of reality *and* the work of transforming that reality – in their dialectical relationship. *It was as if I were saying that to discover reality already meant to transform it.*[70] [emphasis in original]

Although Freire now perceives the dialectical relationship between knowledge and action, echoes of earlier idealism can still be heard. Not to realise that violence in the cause of humanisation will at some stage manifest hatred by the oppressed of their class antagonist, and to simply assert that such violence will initiate love, is to idealise and mythify the reality of revolutionary situations. As he did when discussing leadership, on the subject of violence Freire displays a tendency towards idealism that weakens an otherwise realistic appraisal of political struggle. This same tendency leads him to minimise the crucial significance, for successful revolutions, of the transfer of political power. 'The taking of power,' he writes, 'is only one moment – no matter how decisive – in the revolutionary process'.[71] This needs more explication than Freire provides. By neglecting the political and economic bases of power relations in society Freire parts company with the materialism of Marx. The discussion of liberation and oppression provided by Freire is couched throughout in psychological terms, which, despite their penetration and great force, omit the material and economic bases of social arrangements. Certainly Freire states the crucial question:

> if the implementation of a liberating education requires political power and the oppressed have none, how then is it possible to carry out the pedagogy of the oppressed prior to the revolution?[72]

The problem is that Freire's answer encompasses only the necessary, but not the sufficient grounds for political and cultural revolution. His analysis stipulates the necessary conditions as: the dialectical contradiction between oppressor and oppressed, resulting in class antagonism which can only be resolved, under dialogical leadership, by a violent transformation of the oppressive social reality. In this sense Freire can be seen as a revolutionary socialist. Yet if the sufficient conditions for revolution are also to be provided, he must shed the vestigial idealism which intrudes into several facets of his thought. In particular, ignoring the economic bases of political struggle means that Freire deserts Marx at the very point where Marx is most effective. One political consequence of this is that Freire's radicalism runs the serious risk of evaporating into mere rhetoric, especially if his seminal notions of conscientisation and praxis are deprived of their material base. This is not what Freire would desire, but his idealism could presage precisely this. The liberation his pedagogy is designed to serve has, therefore, its necessary grounds in Freire's formulations. The search for additional, sufficient, grounds is one, at the moment, he refrains from undertaking.

(iv) Existentialism

Whereas Freire's politics have become more radical over time, other elements contributing to his thought, notably ideas stemming from European existentialists, recur constantly throughout his writings. In this connection the personalist philosophy of Emanuel Mounier has already been noted. Freire also draws upon the writings of Martin Buber, Karl Jaspers, Jean-Paul Sartre and Gabriel Marcel to explicate various aspects

115

of his theory. Here, as in other parts of his work, Freire evinces an intellect that is synthetic and broadly eclectic.

Central to Freire's understanding of literacy, politics and education is the term dialogue. This is 'the encounter between people, mediated by the world, in order to name the world'.[73] Dwelling in a culture of silence the oppressed must first regain their right to speak. Dialogue thus becomes an existential necessity.[74] It is a horizontal relationship of mutual trust among the oppressed. Where it is characterised by love, faith, hope, and critical consciousness then dialogue truly communicates. On this point Freire endorses Karl Jaspers directly:

> dialogue is the only way, not only in the vital questions of the political order, but in all the expressions of our being. Only by virtue of faith does dialogue have power and meaning: by faith in man and his possibilities, by the faith that I can only truly become myself when other men also become themselves.[75]

For Freire dialogue is that form of interpersonal relationship between subjects which not only interprets the world, but seeks to transform it. The influences not only of Marx but also of Martin Buber are apparent. Freire does not demur from Buber's observation that 'the relation in education is one of pure dialogue'.[76] Buber's *I-Thou* relationship, however, is conceived by Freire in explicitly dialectical terms:

> the dialogical *I*, however, knows that it is precisely the *thou* . . . which has called forth his own existence. He also knows that the *thou* which calls forth his own existence in turn constitutes and *I* which has in his *I* its *thou*. The *I* and the *thou* thus become, in the dialectic of these relationships, two *thous* which become two *Is*.[77] [emphasis in original]

What Freire is driving at here is an explanation of dialogue from the point of view of the oppressed. When it is recognised that the dominated class have the oppressor 'dwelling within' their consciousness, then dialogue among the oppressed can only transpire when the dominator is distanced and objectified. In short, the oppressed can only perceive how they have been conditioned when they are confronted with problems arising

116

from their existential situation. Freire's literacy programme is largely based on this insight. The recognition of oppression comes from consideration of generative words and themes originating as the collective essence of an oppressive existence. Since consciousness and particularly its fundamental property, intentionality, is Freire's central concern, this further entails commitment to the humanisation of the oppressed – not simply in the form of words, but through active intervention on their side.

Freire is emphatic that the struggle for liberation requires a complete rejection of all forms of oppressive pedagogy. This means a repudiation of the banking concept in its entirety. Where the educator makes deposits of information that 'fill' the student, then this corresponds to what Sartre calls the 'digestive' or 'nutritive' concept of education.[78] Freire's literacy programme is an elaboration and application of Sartre's critique of the notion that 'to know is to eat'. Illiterates are often considered under-nourished, not merely in the physical sense, but also because they lack the 'bread of the spirit'. In this way illiteracy comes to be seen as a disease which must be eradicated. The nutritionist view of education is implicit in literacy campaigns which conceive the illiterate as 'starving for letters, thirsty for words', and so the word is brought to them to assauge this hunger and thirst. Understood in this way, Freire adds, people are merely passive beings, objects of the literacy process and not its subjects.[79]

The influence of existentialism on Freire's thinking is highlighted by the sharp distinction he draws between the banking, or nutritionist, approach to education, and problem-posing:

> in problem-posing education, people develop their power to perceive critically *the way they exist* in the world *with which* and *in which* they find themselves.[80] [emphasis in original]

Where the banking method emphasises permanence and becomes reactionary, problem-posing education is rooted in the dynamic present and is thus revolutionary.[81] 'To be an act of knowing,' Freire affirms, 'the adult literacy process must engage the learners in the constant problematising of their existential

117

situations.'[82] By taking as his starting point human incomple-
tion, and focusing his educational endeavours on both the analysis
and transformation of concrete existence, Freire endeavours to
synthesise christian existentialism with revolutionary politics.

Conclusion: The Eclectic Paulo Freire

The purpose of this chapter has been to sketch in something of an intellectual terrain traversed and inhabited by Paulo
Freire. A study of the manifold sources he draws upon reveals
Freire's development from parochial to universal concerns.
Moreover, it indicates that his is an intellect which is curious,
supple, provocative and self-critical. The undoubted power and
appeal of his theory stems as much from these qualities as it does
from his obvious compassion, sympathy and identification with
the oppressed.

Freire has not built up his theory systematically or
rigorously. Rather it has emerged, and continues to take shape,
through an intense process of action and reflection. The features
highlighted in this discussion are not offered in order of
importance, or appearance. Nor are they perceived as separate,
discrete influences. Others reading Freire could well come to
different conclusions. Indeed the very diversity of his thought is
both a strength and a weakness: a strength in that it creatively
draws together many strands of contemporary thinking into a
dynamic and challenging theory; a weakness, in that such a
procedure makes it all too easy for one aspect of Freire's writing
to be spotlighted at the expense of others. Distortion is an ever-
present danger. The most appropriate solution is to view his
work as a whole, and recognise that Freire's intellect borrows
freely from whatever sources illuminate his central theme:
literacy and revolution.

Evaluations of Freire also need to understand the audience
he is addressing. In *Pedagogy of the Oppressed* and *Cultural
Action for Freedom* he is speaking to and for the oppressed
everywhere. In fact the dedication of his major work, *Pedagogy
of the Oppressed*, states that intention directly. Freire's 'third
world' audience, however, is not located solely among former
colonial territories. Nor is it limited to the so-called under-

118

developed nations of Latin America and South America, Africa or Asia. Freire is explicit that 'the concept of the third world is ideological and political, not geographic'. From this standpoint,

> the so-called 'first world' has within it and against it its own 'third world'. And the third world has its first world, represented by the ideology of domination and the power of the ruling classes. The third world is in the last analysis the world of silence, of oppression, of dependence, of exploitation, of the violence exercised by the ruling classes on the oppressed.[83]

In the light of this conception Freire is seriously misunderstood if it is thought that his pedagogy is only applicable to Brazil or Guinea-Bissau. What began, in *Education: the Practice of Freedom*, as the attempt to identify an emerging Brazilian nationalism with critical consciousness via adult literacy, is now the fundamental theme for the third world – the conquest of its right to a voice. Paulo Freire has only one desire: that his thinking

> may coincide historically with the unrest of all those who, whether they live in those cultures which are wholly silenced or in silent sectors of cultures which prescribe their voice, are struggling to have a voice of their own.[84]

119

8. The End of Dialogue: Paulo Freire on Politics and Education
by Jim Walker

Che Guevara once said: 'If you want an education, join the revolution!' To be sure, he was raising a slogan to recruit guerrillas, not making a heavy theoretical point about the relation between education and politics. Nevertheless, the idea that revolution is a highly educative process is often proclaimed by revolutionaries. Paulo Freire, an admirer of Guevara and an advocate of revolution, certainly holds this opinion, but is as convinced of the revolutionary potential of education as of the educational potential of revolution.

Freire's insistence on the political nature of all education, and most importantly his own example as a practical educator, have drawn worldwide attention to this work. It is probably these aspects of his work rather than others, which have inclined many people to believe that Freire has something to offer which is somehow special, over and above what can be learned from other educational radicals. While he does have a specialised appeal to particular groups, for example radical christians, even this depends usually on his uncompromisingly political approach.

As Freire himself puts it: 'Education is always a political event'.

We might speculate that it is precisely because they have sensed a political threat in Freire that many educational 'experts' have rushed to emasculate his work. By presenting him as if he were contributing exciting new methods of teaching literacy usable by teachers regardless of their politics, they have tended to turn Freire into a respectable educational 'figure' and to domesticate his influence. On the other hand many radicals have tended to see in Freire the promise of a liberating link-up between education and the broader arena of struggle, pointing to a viable politics of emancipation.

120

On one view Freire becomes a literacist for all seasons, on the other a guide to human liberation.

In fact he is neither.

The connection between language and politics is obvious in the third world. The sparking off of the Soweto revolt by the issue of studying in Afrikaans is perhaps the most dramatic recent example. It may not be so obvious in more complex and sophisticated societies lacking such pivotal clashes between cultures, but the subtlety, in a way, makes the tracing of the connection so much the more important.

But this point will not be argued here. Previous chapters have examined Freire on education, and on literacy in particular. Here I shall offer a critique of Freire's politics, and in particular of his understanding of revolution and its relation to his educational practice. Those looking to Freire for political guidance might be surprised at where he leads them, and I shall argue that they should certainly be displeased. There are deep contradictions in Freire, which make the realisation of his basic human ideals unlikely in the context of his politics. Indeed Freire's politics threaten to turn back on and attack the very movement towards humanisation and liberation it is designed to promote.

The fact that education is political is now becoming obvious to more and more students, teachers and parents, in ways that were not possible even a few years ago. For some, like the inhabitants of Soweto, this fact has been a dominant feature of their experience for as long as they can remember, and has recently been seared in to the forefront of consciousness as the violent political reality underlying the South African educational system has been made embarrassingly clear to the whole world. In London, Britain's nazis, the National Front, are organising within schools to restore white pride in the British 'race' and work up 'appropriate' attitudes to children of West Indian, Pakistani and Indian descent. In Britain and Australia voices are heard urging moves to curb 'marxists' in schools and universities (long harassed in numerous other countries) supported by the contradictory argument that there should be political discrimination in education to secure its political neutrality.

Indeed, now that the political nature of education is

increasingly evident, those whose political interests are protected by the established structure of schooling and threatened by revelation of the realities of that structure are faced with two basic alternatives. They can come out into the open and start turning schools into acknowledged centres of political indoctrination along the lines of China, the Soviet Union and other countries where the ruling ideology is clearly taught as such. However, this would mean, for western countries, contradicting the prevailing form of liberal ideology which pretends that no particular 'line' is taught in schools, and it would be countenanced only as a last resort. The other path is rigorous rehabilitation of the idea that education is or should be politically neutral, and that partisan engagement in the schools is out of order. In 1976 teachers in New South Wales were informed by the Director General of Education:

> Schools are neutral grounds for rational discourse and objective study, and should not become arenas for opposing political or other ideologies.[1]

Which means in practice that the ruling ideology should not be opposed. The same line has been taken by authorities in Britain over the moves of the National Front and others.

This neutralist myth will be harder and harder to sustain in the years ahead, as the economic and educational crises deepen; but the establishment seems stuck with it, short of a drastic change towards explicit authoritarianism.

In such circumstances it is all the more important to have educators who not only stress the impossibility of neutrality, and the political character of education, but who can provide explanations of how and why political forces are at work in education, and how liberation from political domination can be achieved. That is, we need both theory and a practical method springing from that theory. Freire attempts both.

In view of Freire's influence, and the urgency of the task in which he claims to be engaged, it is important to understand clearly, if we can, what his views are on the relationship between education and politics. How do they differ from other radical views? How can an educational process be involved in funda-

122

mental, even revolutionary change? What does Freire understand by 'revolution'?

In tackling these questions, I shall try, as Freire would insist we should in all investigations of education, to consider theory and practice, and so far as is possible, to consider them together. In Freire's case, this means looking at his current work in the north-west African country of Guinea-Bissau.

Freire and Radical Education

In the past two decades the west has seen a torrent of more or less popular literature on education, most of it more or less radical. Among the best known thinkers and polemicists have been Paul Goodman, John Holt, Jonathon Kozol, Jules Henry, George Dennison, Ivan Illich and Everitt Reimer.[2] These critics of orthodox education have put modern form and concrete illustrations on objections to schooling which have a long history: that it is dull and boring, alienating, authoritarian, wasteful of resources and human energy, that instead of developing individual ability and potential it blocks them, that instead of fostering social equality it promotes inequality, and so on. As Holt succinctly puts it, 'schools are bad places for kids'. Much the same points, give or take an emphasis here and there, and allowing for an earlier historical context, were made by John Dewey, Albert Einstein, Bertrand Russell and A. S. Neill, and by others in earlier periods. The philosophical and psychological frameworks, the explicit educational theories, and the proposals for change have not always been the same, but the humanistic and liberal values and the specific criticisms of conventional schooling have been broadly similar.

For Dewey, the alternative was changing the form and content of modern education in a more progressive direction; for Russell and Neill it was this and also, if possible, setting up schools outside the established state or church systems. These tendencies have been resurgent recently, and particularly with the wider upheavals in western society in the sixties, have won a wider, though never of course a majority, support. Illich and Reimer, and others in their wake, drew the extreme conclusion in proposing the abolition of all schools as we know them, and their

123

replacement by informal learning webs sited in a more or less free market of learning.[3]

This educational tradition (if we can call it that) has had little formative influence on Freire. He certainly did not interact with it in a practical sense until his own ideas were well past immaturity. He actually engaged it in a significant sense only with Illich and Reimer.[4]

All the same, there are similarities between Freire's ideas and those popularised by radical educators in the west. The damnation he calls down on 'banking' education, with its 'deposits' in passive pupil receptacles is familiar enough, and he shares with many other radicals the value placed on self-directed and self-managed learning, though within a collective setting. Implicitly Freire's insight into the differences between banking and problem-posing education goes beyond other radical views. It could be developed within a wider theory of exchange relations within educational institutions, and between these and other institutions; but something more dialectical than the static 'banking' metaphor would be required to capture the exchange transaction of education. To this is added the explicit political interpretation of education. Because Freire's work began in Brazil and continues among other peoples who have felt the domination of Portuguese imperialism, the political dimension has added cultural significance. The peoples of Brazil, Mozambique, Guinea-Bissau and Angola experienced more in common than the brutality of the Portuguese military (replaced in Brazil by an equally obnoxious local war machine) rapacious landowners, and other extractors of wealth from the labour of subjugated peoples. They experienced invasion and domination by an alien culture, which in turn submerged them in a culture of silence and cemented together the structure of economic, political and military control. The alienation attacked by radicals in western education is alien twice over when, in the colonial or neo-colonial situation, the whole society is conquered from outside.

There have, of course, been political currents among western radical education movements. The radicalisation of some educational thought and practice in the 1960s, especially in the US, was often closely associated with student radicalisation,

124

the campus revolts, and the broader civil rights and peace movements. Many who became involved in radical and alternative education did so for political motives. The demand for student power seemed to them to be on the way to fulfilment in some of the ideas and practices of radical education.

But on the whole the link between radical politics and radical education was at best tenuous. The political bankruptcy of many tendencies in the radical education movement itself became apparent when they were relatively easily seduced by Illich's deschooling gospel, which in practical terms turned out to mean one of two things. First, Illich sometimes said, since schools have made the whole social system so hopeless, all we can do is sit back and wait for it to collapse around us. Then we shall act. This was complete abstentionism: for the present do nothing. As such it gave a rationale for the already widespread drop-out mentality. Or secondly, we could start to organise learning webs and push the policies needed to support them. It turned out that for Illich this meant free enterprise capitalism seemingly indistinguishable from that advocated by reactionary monetarists like Milton Friedman. Either way, the contradictions in Illich, though covered with left-wing rhetoric, led to a betrayal of the radical cause (which is not, of course, to gainsay Illich's many insights into modern industrial society).

Partly in spite of and partly because of the extinguishing of most of the radical political movements of the sixties, there was a revival of interest in political theory, especially various versions of marxism.[5] In this theoretical renaissance, education has gradually come in for some attention. Indeed marxist analysis has sometimes appealed because it seems to explain the educational crisis.[6]

It is against this kind of background that we need to understand Freire's appeal in the west. The fact that he is a voice from the third world adds to his appeal against the background of Vietnam and continued people's revolt in Asia, South America and Africa. True to its contradictory nature, international capital, in indirectly causing Freire to be ejected from first Brazil and then Chile, removed a serpent from its servant's neck, only to have it firmly placed in its own bosom. Freire became celebrated in Harvard and is now based in Geneva!

125

Freire and Marxism

'God led me to the people and the people led me to Marx.'[7]

Like many other christians, especially catholic christians in Latin America, Freire found the social reality around him, which was defended and fostered by the church, completely at odds with his christian faith. And because of the extremes of wealth and poverty, power and powerlessness, luxury and degradation, he became impelled towards a social class understanding of his society. Hence his interest in Marx.

However, unlike orthodox marxists, Freire retains his religious position, and is careful to point out his refusal to accept any incompatibility between this and his attraction to certain marxist ideas:

> When I was a young man, I went to the people, to the workers, the peasants, motivated, really, by my christian faith . . . I talked with the people, I learned to speak with the people – the pronunciation, the words, the concepts. When I arrived with the people – the misery, the concreteness, you know! But also the beauty of the people, the openness, the ability to love which the people have, the friendship . . .

> The obstacles of this reality sent me – to Marx. I started reading and studying. It was beautiful because I found in Marx a lot of things the people had told me – without being literate. Marx was really a genius.

> *But when I met Marx, I continued to meet Christ on the corners of the street – by meeting the people.*[8] [emphasis in original]

This is a vitally important passage for understanding Freire, and captures that essential point of his own experience which is reflected in the central core of his political-educational theory. It would be a mistake to interpret this passage, and Freire's theory generally, as a simple combination of two points of view, christianity and marxism. For example, it has been suggested that Freire engaged in marxist politics and works out

126

marxist theory, but for essentially christian motivation, as if christianity provides the ends and the impetus, while marxism provides the social theory and the political method. In fact, as I shall argue later, christianity provides Freire with more of his social thought and political method, albeit in an existentialist-personalist form, than does marxism. He is, after all, on the staff of the World Council of Churches. This goes somewhat against a common western reaction to Freire, which is expressed in puzzlement as to how a christian can engage in marxist revolutionary politics.

The Politics of Cultural Action

It is worth noting that Freire's most celebrated work as a practical educator has been carried out from positions wherein he has held some power and authority. At the height of his literacy programme in Brazil, he was Secretary of Education and director of an adult education programme for the whole country. It was because of the way he used this power that he was first imprisoned and then exiled by the right after the military coup of 1964. After periods in Bolivia, in Chile (where he became *persona non grata* after the overthrow of Allende) and in the US, he moved to the World Council of Churches, and is now part of an advisory team working in Guinea-Bissau at the government's invitation.

However, his educational practice was not in the first place developed from the perspective of an expert coming to the masses from on high, but through his own struggle to come to terms with the oppressive reality of Brazilian society. He early decided he should identify with the multitudes at the bottom of the rotten festering social heap created by Portuguese imperialism, and perpetuated by an entrenched crypto-colonialism. The process he devised enabled them collectively to gain confidence in their ability to understand their world through their own culture, which very largely had to be re-created in the learning process; and then, in this very learning, to step forward, gaining some control over their world, to be subjects of history rather than objects. All of this came from years of immediate experience with workers and peasants.

127

It was the depth of Freire's experience, and the rootedness of his literacy methods in this experience which commended him to various governments, and which makes a burning impression on all who meet him. It is unfortunate that the abstraction of the writing in parts of Freire's books, and – for non-Portuguese speakers – the fact that they have been translated from the Portuguese, tend to obscure the experimental origins of Freire's theories.[9]

Since the literacy process and most details of the educational theory have been described in earlier chapters, I shall take them as understood, and stick to making a few mainly historical points relevant to the idea of education as a revolutionary process, in Freire's words, as 'cultural action for liberation'. Crucially, the problem facing the countries with which Freire is chiefly concerned has been imperialism, and in education, cultural imperialism.[10] In Brazil, the popular movement was smashed by the reactionaries who secured the continuation of vicious repression and exploitation of the people. As a result Brazil is now a favourite field for investment by western capitalist giants, particularly the United States and West Germany. The developing interdependence between Brazil and West Germany in the nuclear power industry alone goes a long way towards explaining the domination of the people in the interests of western capital and its neo-colonial servants. In Guinea-Bissau, as in the other former Portuguese African colonies of Angola and Mozambique, the story has been somewhat different. The nationalist liberation movements which succeeded in expelling the Portuguese, now form governments of newly independent states, which conceive of themselves as leaders of the masses in the construction of a post-revolutionary society.

Guinea-Bissau is a one-party state: it is ruled by the PAIGC (African Party for the Independence of Guinea and Cape Verde). Although the PAIGC had its rivals they were of no real significance, and it not only led, but virtually created the armed struggle against the Portuguese. In this it was similar to Frelimo in Mozambique, but not the MPLA in Angola which had to struggle against the FNLA and Unita as well as the Portuguese army.

Heading the PAIGC was Amilcar Cabral, one of the most

outstanding of African liberation leaders around whom, since his murder by the Portuguese, legend has already sprung up. On many aspects of life and political struggle in Guinea, Freire is content to let Cabral have the last word, and for the WCC team Cabral is a paradigm of revolutionary leadership:

> Yesterday the liberation struggle. Today, national reconstruction, the building of society free from exploitation and domination. In these common tasks, undertaken by the people and the party, started yesterday, continued today, there is a link, a presence, a constant reference, a face known by all: that of Amilcar Cabral. Many knew him. Almost all have a story of personal experience to tell about him. He is the people's hero and founder of the nation, a friend of everyone.

His memory is an almost mystical Christ-like dimension of present politics:

> the life, death and continued existence of Cabral seals the fusion between Party and People, between old and new, young and old, from which Guinea-Bissau was born.

And the struggle which he led was pre-eminently *cultural and educational:*

> the struggle for liberation is not just a cultural fact, but also a cultural factor . . . PAIGC and the liberation struggle which it initiated were the great teachers, the great educators, of the people.[11]

The Guinea-Bissau experience illustrates clearly the similarities and differences between the two kinds of education of which Freire had written in *Pedagogy of the Oppressed.* There, he asks the question:

> If the implementation of a liberating education requires political power and the oppressed have none, how then is it possible to carry out a pedagogy of the oppressed prior to the revolution?

129

His answer;

> One aspect of the reply is to be found in the distinction between systematic education, which can only be changed by political power, and educational projects, which should be carried out *with* the oppressed, in the process of organising them.[12] [emphasis in original]

These are seen by Freire as two stages in the liberation process. The prime task in the first is the simultaneous unveiling of the world of oppression and the practical struggle to transform it. This is praxis: revelation of the reality of oppression is not possible without action, and revolutionary action is not possible without commitment. In Freire's view, this is where the necessarily political character of all education resides: for either you are learning about the world in the essentially human struggle to transform it, or you are passive, inert, dehumanised and capable only of perceiving the world in the imposed ideology and culture. This is not intended as a static either/or. Naturally there are stages in the development of critical consciousness, or conscientisation, before any really conscious, purposive struggle is pursued. Thus the liberating pedagogy is principally cultural confrontation, resistance to the invading culture and the creation of a culture appropriate to the life of people in control of their work and social world.

But the culture of domination is confronted in the second stage also. Here, after the revolution cultural action becomes continuing cultural revolution, a maximum effort at conscientisation, which reaches all aspects of social life to remold them, and every person. It makes the same assumptions as maoist cultural revolution: the political struggle having been won, further progress now requires

> the expulsion of the myths created and developed in the old order, which like spectres haunt the new structures emerging from the revolutionary transformation.[13]

It is cultural action, then, which unifies both stages of cultural action for liberation.[14] In the first stage it is part of a material, physical struggle against oppressors, that is, action by the oppressed and their leaders. In the second, 'the pedagogy

130

ceases to belong to the oppressed and becomes a pedagogy of *all* the people in the process of permanent liberation' [emphasis in original].[15]

Thus Freire regards the class divisions inherent in oppressive society as obliterated by the nationalist revolution, so that what remains in the struggle is almost entirely cultural. I want presently to raise some problems for this opinion.

To appreciate the stress which Freire places on cultural action in his writings and his current practical work, one should be aware of the severity of cultural domination inflicted by the Portuguese. There is not space here to describe the sometimes stupefyingly brutal oppression by what was, it should be remembered, fascist imperialism.[16] This reached such a peak during the wars of liberation in Angola, Mozambique and Guinea that large sections of the Portuguese army rebelled, no longer able to stomach their role as enforcers in forced labour systems. It is perhaps not widely enough realised that the end of fascism in Portugal was a result of the African liberation struggles, which led to the contradictions of metropolitan Portuguese society eventually exploding in a workers' movement which burst asunder the fabric of fascist rule.

Colonial rule not only imposed political and economic domination, it ruptured the normal learning experiences of the people and hence disintegrated indigenous African culture. 'For the Portuguese . . . "educate" meant "de-Africanise" '.[17] No longer did the child learn by a process of participation in the ongoing life of the family group and the community, gaining skill and understanding of life and work through living and working. No longer were the elders able effectively to pass on tribal wisdom through daily conversation between young and old, nor was the body of traditional beliefs and values, expressed in ritual and ceremony, able to preserve the integrity of the community.

Along with the army, the key institution in the subjugation of black and white was the school. European-style schools, teaching European-style curricula, hideously deformed, had

> no other goal than teaching the Africans how to be more useful to the Portuguese. The colonial army invaded the land and brutalised the physical body, while the colonial

school, its functional counterpart, tamed the mind and domesticated the soul.[18]

As in the west, but in more marked fashion, success at school and the number of years actually spent there, created a system of stratification, a colonial class structure. The vast majority of those entering school received some tiny minimum of primary education, and then went back to their villages to become good hardworking peasants with appropriate feelings of inferiority. They were made well aware that they were unable to go on to secondary education and become part of a newly emerging privileged minority who, having passed the requisite western examinations, moved into professional, semi-professional and managerial positions in the service of their colonial overlords and in distinction from the mass of their fellow Africans. The school system created a colonial petit bourgeoisie. The contradictions in the consciousness of this class were to be crucial for the course taken by the liberation struggle. Unlike the masses, submerged in the 'culture of silence', the black petit bourgeoisie was tempted to see the European culture as its own, to be pulled right away from its African roots. Of course the aspirations that developed were never to be satisfied, and the petit bourgeoisie was left in limbo – in Fanon's words, with black skins and white masks.

As the WCC team sees it, the PAIGC's response in the liberation movement was to confront the programme of domestication with a 'new educational reality'. Their description of PAIGC education at this stage is worth quoting at some length:

> the children were brought together around a member of the PAIGC in a forest clearing, protected from the sun and the Portuguese bombers by branches of trees. In the liberated areas . . . a new school came into being . . . the first lesson consisted of learning how to identify the noise of the planes so as to escape their rain of death.

> The learning process tried to rediscover what had been positive in the experience of the 'traditional' African society. The spontaneity and informality of traditional

132

education was revalorised. So was a return to learning from the experience of the elders. Above all, the learning was done through practice. The very fact that there were great shortages of material resources brought about a necessary relation between learning on the one hand and production and community tasks on the other . . . study was directly related to productive work and the students fully partici- pated in the management of the school and its material upkeep . . . the liberation movement sought to develop . . . a new mentality stripped of the negative aspects and prejudices of the traditional society such as, for example, the inferior position of women in the social structure or the sense of powerlessness against natural phenomena.[19]

But it was not as if an entirely new educational system had fully developed when, after the Portuguese revolution, the colonisers left the country in September 1974. Suddenly finding the whole country depending on it, the PAIGC decided that it had no alternative but to take over the old colonial school system as an emergency measure, and set about reforming it as best it could. Elimination of alien ideology from courses such as history and geography, institution of specific political education, and a degree of student participation in school administration were the first steps before thorough educational planning could get under way.

Such planning led in 1975 to mass literacy campaigns (the illiteracy rate was 90 per cent) which met with mixed success. In some cases, mainly in the army, the learning was related to the immediate work of the learners, and so the soldiers did well. Amongst the civilian population this was generally not the case.

It is in the subsequent literacy campaigns that Freire's WCC team has been playing an important role, and in which his theories and methods, developed in Brazil, have been influential in forming the basis for educational policy and practice. Generative theme theory, learning as part of the transformation of everyday life and social reality, and eventually a thoroughly integrated and collective educational process as part of the building of a society, these principles underlie the work.

Educators and Revolutionary Leaders

For Freire, the same principles govern the roles of both the educator and the revolutionary leader. Indeed, it would not be an exaggeration to say that, apart from the military aspects of the revolutionary leadership he has observed in South America and Africa, he sees it as modelled upon what the role of an educator ideally should be.

In the first place, we need to be clear about Freire's account of the origins of revolutionary leadership. For Freire leaders, at least in third world situations, come from the petit bourgeoisie, and he is explicit that this means they come from 'the social strata of the dominators'.[20] They are typically professionals, intellectuals, who 'renounce' their class origins and join the oppressed. But because they are different, they have to struggle with their origins, and continually resist the temptation to act as exploiters and oppressors themselves.

The transformation is described by Freire as an 'easter experience'. The leaders must 'die as elitists so as to be resurrected on the side of the oppressed, that they be born again with the beings who were not allowed to be'. To be a legitimate leader, the petit bourgeois must 'make his easter'.[21]

This view of the nature of the revolutionary leadership and therefore of the nature of the revolution itself, is the most fundamental point to grasp for an adequate understanding of Freire's view of education and politics. It is what creates the greatest theoretical difficulties for him, and lays him open to charges of cynical totalitarian elitism from sophisticated conservatives.[22] It is also important if we are to see the point of Freire's continual emphasis on dialogue. Tied in with this, it helps to explain how christianity and marxism come together in Freire. Finally it leaves him, I think, little alternative but to model his concept of revolutionary leadership on a particular view of teacher-student relationships.

Freire regards the petit bourgeois nature of the leadership as inevitable; no other possibility is considered in his work. When it comes to Guinea-Bissau, he finds his assumptions completely exemplified, not only in what actually happened, but in the

134

theory developed by Cabral to analyse that society, and guide the liberation struggle. According to Cabral:

> The colonial situation, which does not permit the development of a native pseudo-bourgeoisie and in which the popular masses do not generally reach the necessary level of political consciousness before the advent of the phenomenon of national liberation, offers the petit bourgeoisie the historical opportunity of leading the struggle against foreign domination, since by nature of its subjective and objective position (higher standard of living than the masses, more frequent contact with the agents of colonialism, and hence more chances of being humiliated, higher level of political awareness, etc.) it is the stratum which most rapidly becomes aware of the need to free itself from foreign domination.[23]

The petit bourgeoisie, or a section of it, is therefore revolutionary, and upon it depends the mobilisation of whatever revolutionary possibilities the masses have.

Further, insofar as the revolution is concerned with social equality, or even with socialism, Cabral's view has absolutely drastic implications for the behaviour of the petit bourgeoisie, and demands, once this class is on the way to winning power, the most extraordinary moral commitment and sacrifice. It has to resist becoming bourgeois itself, and this means it must be capable of 'class suicide', and rebirth as 'revolutionary workers'. It seems that this occurs, voluntarily, at the level of ideas and attitudes, by an act of decision originating in moral conviction, and unrelated to any significant feature of historical development in the material structure of society:

> This alternative, to betray the revolution or to commit suicide as a class, constitutes the dilemma of the petit bourgeoisie . . . The positive solution . . . depends on what Fidel Castro recently correctly called *the development of revolutionary consciousness.* This dependence naturally calls our attention to the capacity of the leader . . . to remain faithful to principles and to the fundamental cause of this struggle. This shows us, to a certain extent, that if

national liberation is essentially a political problem, the conditions for its development give it certain characteristics which belong to the sphere of morals.[24] [emphasis in original]

Thus the ideas, consciousness and moral consistency of leaders are made crucial. Like Cabral, Freire cites Castro, as well as Guevara and Mao on this. We should be suspicious of this particular invocation of the power of morality and political significance of moral commitment. For Cabral's advocacy of 'class suicide', and Freire's preaching of 'easter experiences' look very much like ad hoc devices to resolve theoretical dilemmas in the justification of their politics, linked with illusory utopian hopes for a particular line of practical action. They want to have their political cake and eat it too. What precisely is supposed to be happening? Perhaps it is hard to be precise about the account we are being offered, but a reasonable interpretation is that it is describing a mystical transformation of hitherto very materially determined beings, the leadership class, by an act of sheer moral and, in Freire's case religious will.

While this may look ad hoc from a practical political point of view, in the context of Freire's total thoretical perspective it is far from being so. It is an expression of his fundamental existentialist-christian orientation, in this case the idea of a specially sanctioned, self-sacrificial missionary role for the educator-leaders. Unfortunately this makes the case worse than if it were an ad hoc move. The problems are tied to the very core of Freire's theory. Even supposing that it is realistic to preach such a gospel, supposing that the 'sacrificial' class will respond, or even that it is possible for them to respond, it is a further question whether the response will have the political effects expected of it, namely that *sui generis* moral will can cancel out class conflict. There is no evidence that it ever has or ever could. Freire trades on hope rather than prediction, faith rather than expectation and love rather than political realism.

It is on this point that Freire's liberal christianity is most at odds with traditional marxism.[25] According to Marx, the classless society, or as Freire's WCC team puts it, the 'society in which people no longer exploit one another', is possible only through the action of the working class in its struggle to free itself from capitalist exploitation. And although at particular historical stages there may be some temporary coincidence of interests between the working class and the bourgeoisie or the petit bourgeoisie, the working class needs no outside leadership. In fact it can expect nothing but betrayal if it submits to such leadership. Marx put it succinctly in his 'battle-cry': 'The emancipation of the working class must be the work of the working class itself.'[26]

Like Marx, Freire holds that society consists essentially of two antithetical poles: a dominating pole and a dominated pole. Whatever the details of class composition in particular times and places – and the details are constantly changing – for Marx this contradiction can be resolved only dialectically, when the dominated defeat the dominators. This is revolution. But for Freire, revolution requires 'the existence, not only of these poles, but also of a leadership group' which can go either way, and is therefore responsible either for the revolution or its absence.[27] More than this, Freire goes to considerable pains to emphasise how different this group is, by highlighting its duty to die and rise again, by hinting at its sacerdotal and, possibly, messianic significance. For Marx, if the petit bourgeoisie ends up either with, or in the working class, it is because of material economic forces tending to proletarianise the petit bourgeoisie.[28] For Freire, if the petit bourgeoisie ends up on the side of the oppressed it is a result of dialogics: for Marx, of dialectics. In general terms we need a dialectical conception of social change. This does not entail any devaluation of dialogical relations between people, but rather denying the political role assigned to them by Freire which eventually, we shall argue shortly, actually cuts off possibilities for genuine dialogue, insofar as it is wrongheaded about the conditions necessary for equality of communication between people.

Freire's hopes for the petit bourgeoisie are mirrored in a hint of suspicion of the working class. Speaking primarily of Brazil, he comments:

> large sections of the oppressed form an urban proletariat, especially in the more industrialised centres of the country.

Although these sectors are occasionally restive, they lack revolutionary consciousness and consider themselves privileged. Manipulation, with its series of deceits and promises, usually finds fertile soil here.[29]

Like Mao, whom he often quotes in this connection, Freire finds greater revolutionary potential in the peasantry; that is, more likelihood that they will follow the lead of the petit bourgeoisie.

Like Mao, Fanon and many third world revolutionary intellectuals prominent during the 1960s, Freire puts a view of class struggle as determined mainly mechanically by consciousness of oppression. He gives only the sketchiest of accounts of the social roots of such consciousness, and then often forgets about them when discussing conscientisation, or the development of critical consciousness, in a predominantly abstract manner. Now changing consciousness is fine and necessary. But it is not sufficient, and in any case is incapable of proceeding in an emancipatory direction, changing class consciousness independently of changes in the productive relations of society, or to use Marx's metaphor, independently of developments in the material base. Because Freire is at best vague about the nature of that base he winds up with a very abstract treatment of consciousness, and an idealist rather than a materialist account of social change. It is hard to see how a christian could do otherwise.

As we shall see, this leads to illusions about the potential of Freirean style revolution to provide the economic conditions necessary for a non-exploitative society.

In Freire's account, the revolutionary leaders have to change two kinds of consciousness: their own and that of the oppressed. Anxious to avoid a repeat of the same old manipulation and exploitation exercised by the oppressors, Freire builds up an elaborate theory of dialogue and communication to bridge the gap between leaders and people. Anxious to avoid charges of elitism, he tries to show the dialogical process as progressively blurring differences between the groups, so that they become 'equally the subjects of revolutionary action' and 'actors in communication'.[30] In just what sense the 'teacher-learner-leaders' and the 'learner-teacher-people' are equal remains obscure.

138

Nor is equality really likely to happen within Freire's political framework. One might expect the people to be given power of some sort over their leaders, but democracy does not figure in the theory of dialogue. Although Freire endorses the formalisation of political power in parties such as the PAIGC, the emphasis always remains on how the petit-bourgeois leaders can work with the people, and lead them along the right path. They remain pedagogues, but dialogical pedagogues, not monological. In fairness we should note that Freire asserts that leaders should not fear the people, and should be accountable to the people, but leaves it up to the leaders to decide how this is to be done, so long as it is compatible with dialogue. They must make themselves the people's comrades:

> in thinking about the people in order to liberate [rather than dominate] them, the leaders give of themselves to the thinking of the people. One is the thinking of the *master*; the other is the thinking of the comrade.[31] [emphasis in original]

Thus the essence of a Freirean relationship between leaders and people is dialogue. Again, of course, it is the leaders who initiate this dialogue. Freire speaks as if the revolution itself were separate from the people. It must speak with them. His worries about the ethics of revolutionaries, and the problem of distinguishing between their actions and the manipulations of the oppressors, are here, as in many other places, very evident.

> Sooner or later, a true revolution must initiate a courageous dialogue with the people. Its very legitimacy lies in that dialogue.[32]

Presumably, if the people have already made the revolution or even participated in it, as Freire – inconsistently with the idea we are considering here – seems to think they should, demand for this dialogue would be otiose, indeed self-contradictory. Although Freire is confused: he says both that the legitimacy of a revolution lies in its dialogical character (a normative question) and that it is such dialogue which distinguishes a revolution from a military coup (a conceptual question). He does not mention, in distinguishing either between legitimate and illegitimate revolutions, or between revolutions and coups, the kinds of changes in social relations which the one might be expected to bring about in contrast to the other – like workers' control of factories, farms and offices. His emphasis is not upon these bedrock social realities, but upon communion, trust and dialogue. Now of course the point of revolution might well be to fill the world with communion, trust and dialogue, among other things. Indeed, the demand for a change in the mode of production is largely for the sake of these, and the freedom and equality which they presuppose. But this is completely different from defining revolutions or marking off legitimate ones from the rest, where the crucial questions concern not dialogue, but power and who has it. The relevant point here is that the way Freire draws the distinctions is no accident given his theory, as distinct perhaps from certain aspects of his practice. And in view of Freire's insistence on the unity of theory and practice, this is no purely theoretical point, but is of practical political significance.

Again, our attention is drawn to Freire's existentialist christianity. Much modern christian theology has drawn on the personalism of Buber, and on the ideas of Sartre and others for notions hinging largely on the use of the concept of authenticity. The decisively christian framework for action is erected when Freire speaks of the 'easter experience', with its suggestions of death to the old life and resurrection on a higher level of being; and of 'conversion' to the people, which with its christian connotations betokens repentance and the following of a worthy code where others are placed ahead of oneself. All this, of course, within an overall context where salvation is conceived as 'becoming more human', or, as Freire calls it, 'humanisation'. Repentance assumes guilt; moral conduct assumes some motivating cause. In the crucifixion Christ took the guilt (or in existentialist terms, limited humanity) of others on himself. The question to be asked, of course, for the petit bourgeois leadership, is what is guilt, and what is the cause? The conversion leads to a missionary vocation, in which the enlightened reach out to the unenlightened. To press the model further as hostile critics of Freire have done, and to attribute to Freire belief in the moral superiority of the leaders over the unregenerate and less than fully human masses would be unfair.[33] But it would also be unfair to both Freire and the 'people' not to point out the dangers of his line of thought.

In Freire's dialogical theory, there is a necessity for the leadership to enter into communion with the people. This is implicitly, though not explicitly, modelled on the christian notion of communion with God. As Freire says, he continues to 'meet Christ on the corners of the street', by meeting the people. This communion then achieves a mystical 'fusion between leaders and people', which can happen 'only if revolutionary activity is really human, empathetic, loving, communicative and humble, in order to be liberating'.[34] No one would dispute the desirability of these qualities. But do they, and also others we might value – such as consistency, boldness and courage – arise from an act of will, which is really a utopian idea apparently subscribed to by Freire as a christian, or from a concrete historical process? Freire's utter lack of any concrete societal analysis in the development of this theory, that is, his abstraction, leads one to conclude it must be the former. His insistence that leaders must go to the people in a spontaneously dialogical manner reinforces this conclusion.

This conclusion is borne out if we look at the historical precedents to which Freire appeals as exemplifying this theory. Extended exposition and endorsement of the ideas and strategies of Fidel Castro and Che Guevara occupy many pages of his writings. In making out that Castro and his band had the 'dialogical' approach, and not the 'anti-dialogical' approach of manipulators, Freire claims that Fidel 'identified with the people'.[35] Without wishing to shift the discussion to the politics of Mao, Castro and others, we may quite reasonably note, since Freire esteems them so highly and makes use of their ideas, that his estimate of their politics is to say the least controversial, within marxist circles as much as without.

For example, a good case can be made out for a flat denial that Castro and his band identified with the people, for claiming that on the contrary they isolated themselves from the majority of the people when they took to the hills, so much so that when they came to power they had to base themselves on anti-popular elements. One could argue that Guevara's final days as a guerilla revealed his complete severance from the people. And indeed that when Mao finally entered Shanghai, victorious over Chiang Kai Shek and the nationalists, far from being at the head of the people he told the urban workers to keep out of his way, and as soon as things settled down to get back to work under new management. One could at least doubt whether in any of these cases the working class had anything *positive* to do with the success or failure of the revolutionaries.

Freire himself notes that if the communion he asserts must exist does not in fact exist, 'We do see dichotomy: leaders on the one side, and people on the other, in a replica of the relations of oppression'.[36] If he is wrong about the figures he admires, the conclusion he must draw as to the nature of the regimes they have built is obvious. More importantly, there are implications for his estimate of his present work in Africa.

The feeling of need to shore up one's faith in the people is evident in Freire's over-solicitous caution that he might be demeaning them. Over-solicitous because his caution is mis-directed: it ought to be directed elsewhere. For example, in an unconvincing attempt to synthesise 'scientific' and 'humanist' politics Freire writes:

> Scientific and humanist revolutionary leaders . . . cannot believe in the myth of the ignorance of the people. They do not have the right for a single moment to doubt that it is only a myth.[37]

Apart from being inconsistent with other things Freire says, this is simply a mistake. The people are ignorant. So is the petit bourgeoisie. Because of the ideological thralldom in which we live, we all need to struggle for knowledge. Some, such as those whom Freire calls 'intellectuals', have, because of advantages of one sort or another, been able to acquire theoretical knowledge of a certain sort. This carries with it the potential ability to analyse society in more general fashion, for which you might have the opportunity at college or university for example, but not so much on a production line, down a coal mine, or in a rice paddy. Inversely, of course, knowledge of the concrete specifi-cities of oppression is easier to come by in these latter places. But as anyone familiar with higher education can testify, such ability

142

fails to materialise far more often than not. Both the extent of our ignorance and the privileges of some of us are good reasons why we need a liberating politics and a thorough democratisation of society. Hesitating in premature guilt about whether 'we' the 'leaders' are unjustifiably looking down on 'them', the people, simply obscures these facts. It is not elitist to be frank, forthright and realistic. It is essential that knowledge and experience be shared, and built upon in a co-operative and collective fashion. Freire would be quick to agree of course, but he would be clearer about the implications if he were not theoretically locked into the petit-bourgeois intellectual-leader/worker-peasant-oppressed-masses dichotomy. It is not elitist to recognise that intellectuals can make a specific kind of contribution to the struggle, provided it is not assumed that this is part and parcel of a necessarily leadership role. It is not elitist to recognise the prevalence of ignorance. Freire above all, were it not for this side of his theory, knows how cultural invasion produces an oppressed consciousness, including lack of knowledge. It is elitist to believe that the people are not capable of learning, that they are stupid. Or even that they are incapable of organising themselves without the leadership of intellectuals.

The same inconsistency becomes clear when Freire is dealing with 'trust' and its role in dialogue. On the one hand it is 'necessary to trust in the oppressed' to achieve the revolutionary praxis.[38] On the other hand, Freire praises Che Guevara's exhortation that the revolutionary be 'always mistrustful of the people', and comments that this is 'not disregarding the theory of dialogical action', but 'merely being a realist'.[39] Freire tries quite unsuccessfully to reconcile the ideal world of his dialogical revolution with the real world of class struggle, by drawing a distinction which is at odds with nearly all he says elsewhere about dialogue: 'Although trust is basic to dialogue, it is not on a priori condition of the latter . . .'.[40] The reality forcing Freire in to this contradiction is clear enough:

> As long as the oppressor 'within' the oppressed is stronger than they themselves are, their natural fear of freedom may lead them to denounce the revolutionary leaders . . .[41]

Trustful revolutionary leaders, watch out! Again, there is a chasm between idealised ethics and clear-headed politics.

Further, although Freire notes differences between the urban proletariat and the peasantry, for example, for practical purposes 'the people' are taken to be a homogeneous mass. But of course they are not, they are themselves made up of different classes and layers, among whom there is a degree of conflict. This being so, one has to come up with a method of proceeding which recognises this fact, and of explaining how 'unity of the people' is to be achieved. It would be absurd to require of Freire a full-scale social class analysis, which applied across various nations. On the other hand, Freire does offer a universal approach, at least for third world countries: unity imposed by the leadership of the petit bourgeoisie which, having died unto itself and risen again with the oppressed will act as a leaven to unify and purify these other lumps. This reflects populist, rather than socialist politics. Even with an approach based upon dialogue between equals – which would often be far from a realistic possibility – Freire could have made proposals more likely to lead to a humane, non-exploitative society. But what is really needed is a thorough analysis of possibilities based on some concrete understanding of the interplay of social forces. Otherwise universal prescriptions are based on a priori abstractions.

Very rarely does Freire try to analyse the tensions in society in terms of the material conflicts between social classes. He often gives us very interesting social-psychological analyses of oppressor-oppressed situations, but these tend to remain in abstract unrelatedness to actual historical situations. Admittedly, this is a generalisation, but it is a reasonable and fair one.

Nationalism, Socialism and Populism

Freire supports the subordination of the struggle for socialism to another, first priority: the struggle for national independence and cultural freedom. He of course would tend to identify the two struggles; and they of course are undeniably related. The question is how. This means an alliance of classes against the common enemy, imperialism. In third world countries it tends to mean two additional things.

First, because the peasantry is still the overwhelming

144

majority of the population, the struggle becomes oriented around the peasants: they have the only physical power sufficient for removing the imperialists. Second, to the extent that the petit bourgeoisie's interests are thwarted by the imperial power, it has an interest in leading an all-class alliance in an independence struggle. What, though, when formal political independence has been won? From a Freirean point of view, the only possibility seems to be Cabral's conclusion, except of course the possibility of the petit bourgeoisie becoming the new ruling class. The petit bourgeoisie must commit suicide as a class; it must have a collective 'easter experience'. That individual, former petit bourgeois must remain leaders nevertheless is rationalised by Cabral in populist ideology, by making the party the custodian of the will of the people. As Freire's WCC team puts it, the party of liberation in Guinea-Bissau, the PAIGC, is the 'great educator' of the people. For Cabral, the people must find their political existence and expression through the party, and develop under its tutelage, 'because of the economic and cultural limitations of the working masses'.[42] In Angola and Mozambique this ideology has been used to justify suppression of independent working class action, by putting down strikes. Some theoretical remarks by Freire suggest that he might want to reject such a tutelage theory, but the general direction of his politics points towards it, and in Guinea-Bissau he is supporting it in practice.[43]

The political dangers in this flow from the illusions in the theory of revolution we have been examining. First, the need of the 'people' for a leadership elite is justified by the 'limitations' of the people – limitations about which Freire is confused. Second, the legitimacy of the party is grounded in the special qualities of enlightenment and morality of the leadership, and their capacity for and fidelity to dialogue. Hence, incidentally, personality cults – Mao, Fidel, Che, and the mystical veneration already apparently accorded Cabral – 'the life, death and continued existence of Cabral seals the fusion between party and people, between old and new, young and old, from which Guinea-Bissau was born'. Finally despite the rhetoric of liberation, the freedom of the people is vested in the authority of the party, which becomes their only vehicle of expression. Democratic controls, freedom to organise, and education outside the control of the party can have little more than a nominal place in this system.

The contradictions in Freire's theoretical enterprise, within the context of subordination of all basic social functions to the processes of a single organisation, the party, produce the negation of some of his most basic ideals. Freire senses these dangers of course, in his expressed fear of the threat of bureaucracy; but what remedies are suggested by his orientation? More moral attentiveness and application to duty on the part of the leaders, and more conscientisation of the oppressed by the leaders. We are not only moving in a circle, we are trapped in it. The tighter it gets, the more like puritanism and the less like liberation our new position will seem. The process of conscientisation, conceived as the development of collective self management by the oppressed, becomes entangled in parasitic contradictions when other Freirean ideas are realised in practice. Conscientisation as cultural action for liberation is ultimately impossible unless the implicitly authoritarian model of political leadership is jettisoned along with its christian rationalisation, and the development of critical consciousness is not seen as dependent on the subordination of all learning processes to the party. The unity of theory and practice does not entail political domination by one organisation. As Freire argues so thoroughly, conscientisation occurs through dialogue. Dialogue however, depends on some measure of real political equality between participants, not just equality in spirit or in principle, and certainly not just on the good will, good intentions and self sacrifice of the leadership. Freire's own warnings of false generosity are relevant in this connection.

The primacy of the petit-bourgeois-led anti-imperialist struggle means that before and after the revolution, the movement for socialism, for a classless society has to be postponed, seen as a later stage, preceded by populism. Since in Guinea-Bissau and to a lesser extent in the other Portuguese colonies the working class was and is tiny, there were pressures towards populism, and the populism adopted led naturally to a focus on the countryside during the independence struggles. In fact, in Guinea-Bissau Cabral maintained that there was no proletariat as such. However, there were urban workers, and he regarded the majority of these wage earners as committed to the liberation

146

struggle. In focusing on the countryside, however, Cabral was not intending any denigration of the urban worker; on the contrary, he saw clearly that the urban experience was more radicalising than the peasant experience, because urban workers and professionals could see immediately the disparity between their wages and those paid to Europeans for exactly the same work.[44]

The rural guerilla strategy worked in getting rid of the Portuguese. Has it, though, formed the basis for 'building a society where people no longer exploit one another'? We have already noted the chief issue in answering this question: namely the role of the intellectual elite as conducted through the party, the PAIGC. We have expressed doubt as to the realism of Freire's and Cabral's essentially ethical and moralistic view of how class barriers are to be removed. Nor do earlier third world precedents give any grounds for optimism. In China and Cuba for example, the ruling party has become a new ruling class which, whatever the good or bad intentions, exploits the people and limits their powers of organisation in a perfectly straightforward sense.[45] While this is dressed up in marxist terminology and may initially have been and may even now be motivated by noble aspirations on the part of leaders, while there may have been improvements in material conditions of life of the people, and while there may be some worker participation in management – all of which are to be found in varying degrees in the west also – the form of society which has emerged is not socialism, but a highly bureaucratised and disciplined state capitalism.

Freire is aware of the dangers of the wrong kind of society emerging from the practices and politics with which he is involved. However, he is much more concerned about bureaucracy than capitalism. The big danger, for him, is that the revolution might degenerate, 'cease to be a revolution and become a sclerotic bureaucracy'. We noted above that post-revolutionary cultural revolution is considered necessary, because the new order is threatened by lingering 'myths' which must be expelled. Bureaucracy is supposed to threaten because of a failure of consciousness on the part of the leaders. This is Castro's and Cabral's diagnosis as well. The threat bureaucracy constitutes to the new society is located in its manipulative qualities; and it is these same manipulative qualities which lead Freire to oppose populism, without himself escaping it. But what Freire does not take into account is the material basis for populism, which in the case of Guinea-Bissau and of Brazil is economic backwardness. In the cases of Russia and China backwardness led, because of the isolation of these countries, to the application of the 'socialism in one country' doctrine, first promulgated by Stalin in his reversal of the original internationalist tendencies of the Russian revolution and the defeat of any hopes for the kind of socialism envisaged by earlier marxists emerging out of that revolution. The doctrine, so far as it was successfully implemented, reinforced the isolation, and with it bureaucracy and populism.

In the third world, 'socialism in one country' tends to be housed in a theoretical framework which ignores imperialism's role in the world capitalist economic system. Hence, in Freire imperialism is seen as bad primarily because of the cultural domination it entails. The problems of the west are also seen as cultural: it suffers from 'a malaise, a discontent, reflected in a search for fleeting happiness', 'a sensation of having all power and wanting nothing or wanting something which is already lost and gone forever'.[46] Just who has all power in the west is a question rarely raised in such contexts, because there is never any attempt to analyse the west, or Russia, China or Cuba in social class terms. The implication is that the capitalist roots of oppression in the third world are left unconsidered and the political solution to that oppression is seen as strictly an internal question. The inter-relation of events in Portugal and its former African colonies has been sufficient to indicate the inadequacies of this approach. The future and fate of the working classes in the industrial heartlands of the world economic system are not seen as tied in with the fate of Guinea-Bissau, where all hope is invested in national economic independence.

That both Freire and the PAIGC are committed to the doctrine of socialism in one country is quite clear. Section VI of the PAIGC programme is headed 'Economic independence, structuring the economy and developing production'.[47] It speaks of nationalisation, modernisation and rapid development of all resources, particularly agricultural, and the progressive estab-

148

lishment of state commercial and industrial enterprises. As the WCC document puts it, what must be avoided at all costs is 'the recreation of dependence on the outside world'.[48] This is all justified in terms of what the PAIGC calls 'government by the principles of democratic socialism'.[49]

In *Pedagogy of the Oppressed,* Freire writes of the necessity for a liberated society to become a 'being for itself'. This is to be achieved after breaking the 'principal contradiction', which is the 'relationship of dependence between it and the metropolitan society'.[50] He does not explain how primary product exporting Brazil can exercise self-sufficiency in a capitalist world market. Brazil's present rulers have a clearer grasp of that country's economic position, having introduced industrialisation based on high rates of exploitation of labor power and a deeper dependence on foreign capital. Nor does the PAIGC explain how it is going simultaneously to achieve economic independence and provide the material basis for liberation. Even if equality were to be achieved in Guinea-Bissau, an 'equality of poverty' is no use, since, as Marx long ago pointed out, in such a situation only want is generalised. And as Freire knows only too well, scarcity is the origin of competition, and thus of ruling classes and alienation – in a word, of capitalism.

Thus the drive for economic independence has as its main assumption that the chief conflict in the world is, in Freire's words, between 'oppressor' and 'oppressed' nations. Setting aside theoretical objections we might have to his assumption, we can simply point out that it is extremely dubious whether the drive has the faintest chance of success. China, while maintaining the rhetoric of independence, is now set on a course of reintegration into the world economy, after a failure of just those politics which Mao's cultural revolution, in many respects a model for Freire's, was designed to reimplant throughout Chinese society. Predictably, part of the course is a marked swing to the right in educational policy: exams, elites, streaming, scrapping of the 'living, learning and working' educational method which Freire advocates. Much more powerful African states than Guinea-Bissau, such as Tanzania and Zambia, have long since given up the drive. Economic reality, in the shape of a fall in the price of copper, has even forced Kenneth Kaunda of

149

Zambia into collaboration with that quintessential symbol of white imperialism, the regime in South Africa. More recently economic nationalists like Samora Machel in Mozambique and Robert Mugabe in Zimbabwe have abandoned much of the ideological pretence to socialism and have moved to a rapprochement with imperialism.[51] What chance has Guinea-Bissau?

Conclusion

This critique has concentrated on the way in which Freire's theory intermeshes with broad political concerns, rather than focusing on his educational ideas and methods as such. The origin and theory of the revolutionary tradition in which he stands have been located principally in two places: the theory and practice of national liberation movements and the doctrine of socialism in one country on the one hand; and on the other a form of existentialist christianity which gives Freire his theory of how the revolutionary movement is to be conducted, and how it can maintain its moral and political legitimacy. Of these two strands, the latter is the more fundamental for Freire's own conscious practice, but only becomes effective in any concrete sense in the nationalist framework into which it is systematically interwoven. Freire stands clearly in the broad catholic tradition of syncretism, of synthesising christianity with various other theoretical and practical elements to preserve the relevance and influence, of the church through different periods of history and different cultures. South America has been a strikingly fertile part of the world for this tradition.

For Freire, education is 'revolutionary' if it is part of the process of national liberation and its attendant cultural revolution. However much we might support these as general objectives, what needs to be shown in Freire's case is that his theory and practice have the liberating potential he so strongly seeks. This chapter has attempted an analysis of the core of Freire's position considered as political theory and practice. It has suggested that Freire's praxis does not have the liberating potential it aspires to; rather there are dangers that its potential might be the reverse.

150

References

1. Introduction

1. No satisfactory biography of Paulo Freire has yet been published, and the information presented here is compiled from a wide variety of sources including: internal references within Freire's works; Richard Shaull, 'Foreword', in Paulo Freire, *Pedagogy of the Oppressed,* New York: Continuum Books; Emanuel de Kadt, *Catholic Radicals in Brazil,* London: Oxford University Press 1970, pp. 102-107; Jack Shallcrass, 'The politics of education', in *New Zealand Listener,* 13 April 1974; Ian Lister, 'Towards a pedagogy of the oppressed', in *The Times Higher Education Supplement,* 13 July 1973; various articles in *Dialogue,* vol. 7 no. 1, April 1973, particularly T. G. Sanders, 'The Paulo Freire method – literacy training and conscientization', *ibid.* pp.19-31, and in *Dialogue,* vol.8 no.2, August 1974; and interview with Barry Hill, 'When I met Marx I continued to meet Christ on the corner of the street', in *The Age* newspaper, Melbourne: 19 April 1974; 'Paulo Freire talks a little of his life', in *The Open Book,* no.3 1974, pp.10-14, from which the remarks directly quoted in this account derive; and Paul Hodges, 'A voice in silence', in *The New Internationalist,* August 1977, pp.12-13.
2. This edition was published in London: Sheed and Ward 1974, and republished as *Education: The Practice of Freedom,* London: Writers and Readers Publishing Cooperative 1976.
3. See: 'Pilgrims of the obvious', in *Risk,* vol.II no.1, 1975, pp.42-45.
4. Paulo Freire, *Pedagogy in Process: The Letters to Guinea-Bissau,* London: Writers and Readers Publishing Cooperative 1978.
5. Bruce Boston, 'Paulo Freire: Notes of a loving critic', in Stanley M. Grabowski (ed.), *Paulo Freire: A Revolutionary Dilemma for the Adult Educator,* Syracuse New York: ERIC Clearing House on Adult Education 1972.
6. Clift Wright, 'Paulo Freire – What is the importance of his pedagogy for Australia?' in *Cold Comfort,* vol.3 no.1, April 1974.
7. John Elias, *Conscientisation and Deschooling,* Philadelphia: The Westminster Press 1977.
8. See Stanley M. Grabowski, *op.cit.*
9. Cynthia Brown, *Literacy in Thirty Hours: Paulo Freire's Literacy Process in North East Brazil,* London: Writers and Readers Publishing Cooperative 1975.
10. Carol and Lars Berggren, *The Literacy Process: A Practice in Domestication or Liberation,* London: Writers and Readers Publishing Cooperative 1975.

151

11. Martin Hoyles (ed.), *The Politics of Literacy*, London: Writers and Readers Publishing Cooperative 1977.
12. Peter Berger, *Pyramids of Sacrifice*, Penguin 1977.
13. Joel Spring, *A Primer of Libertarian Education*, New York: Free Life Editions 1975.
14. Denis Gleeson. 'Theory and practice in the sociology of Paulo Freire', in *Universities Quarterly*, vol.28 no.3, 1974.

2. Imperialism, Underdevelopment and Education

1. Robert Arnove, 'Education and political participation in rural areas of Latin America', in *Comparative Education Review*, vol.17, no.2, June 1973, p.200.
2. Miguel Arraes, *Brazil: The People and the Power*, Penguin 1972, p.31.
3. Peter Evans, 'Continuities and contradictions in the evolution of Brazilian dependence', in *Latin American Perspectives*, vol.III no.2, p.42.
4. Josue de Castro, *Death in the North East*, New York: Vintage Books 1969, p.115.
5. *ibid*: p.98.
6. Arraes, *op.cit.* p. 56.
7. de Castro, *op.cit.* p.134.
8. *ibid.* p.114. Many writers have used the word 'feudal' to describe the Brazilian landlord–peasant relationship. While this notion correctly conveys the relations of domination involved, it is incorrect in more fundamental ways. The Brazilian landlord has none of the obligations to his serfs accepted by the feudal seigneur, and is himself very much part of the capitalist system of production. Hence the labourer is exposed to the insecurity of unemployment in a way unknown to the genuinely feudal peasant, and has little or no subsistence economy to fall back on when he is retrenched. With no stake in the land he possesses only the dubious resource of labour power.
9. See: Thomas Skidmore, *Politics in Brazil 1930-1964: An Experiment in Democracy*, New York: Oxford University Press 1967.
10. Arraes, *op. cit.* p. 70.
11. Emanuel de Kadt, *Catholic Radicals in Brazil*, London: Oxford University Press 1970, p.46.
12. Arraes, *op.cit.* p.218.
13. Francisco Weffort, 'State and mass in Brazil', in Irving Horowitz (ed.), *Masses in Latin America*, New York: Oxford University Press 1970.
14. Thomas Skidmore, 'Brazil – From revolution to miracle', in C. Harding and C. Roper (eds.), *Latin American Review of Books 1*, California: Ramparts Press 1974, p.107.
15. Anisio Teixeira, 'The changing role of education in Brazilian society', in John Saunders (ed.), *Modern Brazil: New Patterns and Developments*, Gainsville: University of Florida Press 1971, p.82.
16. Arnove, *op.cit.* p.204.
17. *ibid.* p.203.
18. Paulo Freire, *Education: The Practice of Freedom*, London: Writers and Readers Publishing Cooperative 1976, p.19.

3. The Politics of Literacy

1. Martin Hoyles (ed.), *The Politics of Literacy*, London: Writers and Readers Publishing Cooperative 1977, p.29.
2. Paulo Freire, *Education: The Practice of Freedom*, London: Writers and Readers Publishing Cooperative 1976, p.42.
3. *ibid.* p.52.
4. *ibid.* p.46.
5. *ibid.* p.47. The pictures that appear in this volume are those by Vincente de Abreu. The originals by Brenand were confiscated from Freire after the coup in 1964.
6. *ibid.* p.48.
7. *ibid.*
8. Paulo Freire, 'By learning they can teach', in *Studies in Adult education* (Tanzanie) no.2, September 1971, p.82.
9. Paulo Freire, *Cultural Action for Freedom*, Penguin 1972, p.18.
10. Carol and Lars Berggren, *The Literacy Process: A Practice in Domestication or Liberation*, London: Writers and Readers publishing Cooperative 1975, p.28.
11. *ibid.* p.25.
12. *ibid.* p.28.
13. Paul Hodges, 'A voice in the silence', in *The New Internationalist*, August 1977, p.13.
14. Paulo Freire, *Education: The Practice of Freedom, op.cit.* p.34.
15. Wayne O'Neil, 'Properly literate', in Martin Hoyles, *op.cit.* p.73.
16. *ibid.* p.76.
17. *ibid.*
18. Sylvia Ashton-Warner, *Teacher*, New York: Simon and Schuster 1963.
19. Ken Worpole, 'Beyond classroom walls', in Martin Hoyles, *op.cit.* p. 198.
20. Cynthia Brown, *Literacy in Thirty hours: Paulo Freire's Literacy Process in North East Brazil*, London: Writers and Readers Publishing Cooperative 1975, p.36.
21. Harold Rosen, 'Out there, Or where the masons went', in Martin Hoyles, *op.cit.* p.203.

5. Freire, Praxis and Education

1. Paulo Freire, *Cultural Action for Freedom*, Penguin 1972, p.82.
2. Denis Goulet, 'Introduction', in Paulo Freire, *Education: the Practice of Freedom*, London: Writers and Readers Publishing Cooperative 1976, p.ix.
3. Manfred Stanley, 'Literacy: The Crisis of a Conventional Wisdom', in *School Review*, vol.80 no.3, May 1972, p.64.
4. Paulo Freire, *Education: The Practice of Freedom, op.cit.* p.43.
5. Paulo Freire, *Pedagogy of the Oppressed*, Penguin 1972, pp.46-47.

6. Knowledge, Action and Power

1. Paulo Freire, *Education: The Practice of Freedom*, London: Writers and Readers Publishing Cooperative 1976, p.99.
2. Paulo Freire, *Cultural Action for Freedom*, Penguin 1972, p.31.
3. *ibid.* p.35.
4. Norbert Hanson, *Patterns of Discovery*, Cambridge University Press 1972, p.7.
5. Paulo Freire, *Education: The Practice of Freedom, op.cit.* p.134.
6. *ibid.* p.146.
7. Mao Tse-tung, *Four Essays on Philosophy*, Peking: Foreign Languages Press 1968, pp.2-3.
8. Paulo Freire, *Cultural Action for Freedom, op.cit.* p.31.
9. *ibid.* p.33.
10. *ibid.* p.34.
11. *ibid.* p.37.
12. Paulo Freire, *Education: The Practice of Freedom, op.cit.* p.124.
13. Paulo Freire, *Cultural Action for Freedom, op.cit.* p.33.
14. Paulo Freire, *Education: The Practice of Freedom, op.cit.* p.44.
15. *ibid.* p.44, p.110. See also Paulo Freire, 'Education, liberation and the church', in *Study Encounter*, vol.9 no.1, 1973, p.4.

7. Contributions to the Thought of Paulo Freire

1. Paulo Freire *Education: The Practice of Freedom*, London: Writers and Readers Publishing Cooperative 1976, p.40.
2. *ibid.* p.28.
3. *ibid.* p.8.
4. *ibid.* p.38.
5. *ibid.*
6. *ibid.* pp.36, 38.
7. *ibid.* p.29.
8. *ibid.* p.41.
9. *ibid.* p.36.
10. *ibid.* p.18.
11. *ibid.* pp.18-19.
12. *ibid.* p.58.
13. *ibid.* p.10.
14. *ibid.* p.11.
15. Paulo Freire, 'Education, liberation and the church', in *Study Encounter*, vol.9, no.1, 1973, p.1.
16. Paulo Freire, 'Theology of liberation', in *Thinking with Paulo Freire*, a series of tapes made during Freire's visit to Australia in 1974 and available from the Australian Council of Churches, 199 Clarence Street, Sydney, NSW, Australia.
17. Quoted in Emanuel de Kadt, *Catholic Radicals in Brazil*, London: Oxford University Press 1970, p.86.

18. *ibid.*
19. Paulo Freire, *Pedagogy of the Oppressed,* New York: Continuum Books, pp. 135-136. See also *Education: The Practice of Freedom, op.cit.* p. 16.
20. Emanuel de Kadt, *op.cit.* p.84.
21. *ibid.* p.86.
22. *ibid.* p.87-88.
23. Paulo Freire, *Cultural Action for Freedom*, Penguin 1972, p.53.
24. ibid. p.52.
25. *ibid.* pp.54-56.
26. Emanuel de Kadt, *op.cit.* p.92.
27. *ibid.* pp.93-94.
28. *ibid.* p.92.
29. Paulo Freire, *Pedagogy of the Oppressed, op.cit.* p.123
30. *ibid.* p.65.
31. Paulo Freire, 'Education, liberation and the church', *op.cit.* pp.2-3
32. Paulo Freire, 'Naive and shrewd christians', in *Thinking with Paulo Freire, op.cit.*
33. Emanuel de Kadt, *op.cit.* pp.93, 98, 102-107, 236-244.
34. *ibid.* p.98.
35. *ibid.* pp.104-107.
36. *ibid.* pp.90-91.
37. Paulo Freire, *Pedagogy of the Oppressed, op.cit.* p.43.
38. Emanuel de Kadt, *op.cit.* pp.99-101, 104.
39. See two books by Erich Fromm, *Socialist Humanism,* New York: Doubleday 1965; and *Marx's Concept of Man*, New York: Frederick Ungar 1961.
40. Paulo Freire, *Cultural Action for Freedom, op.cit.* p.82.
41. Paulo Freire, *Pedagogy of the Oppressed, op.cit.* p.166.
42. *ibid.* p.31.
43. *ibid.* p.45. Freire is quoting directly here from Erich Fromm, *The Heart of Man,* London: Routledge and Kegan Paul 1966.
44. *ibid.* p.64.
45. Albert Memmi, *The Coloniser and the Colonised*, London: Souvenir Press 1974, p.xvii.
46. *ibid.* pp.88-89.
47. *ibid.* p.20.
48. *ibid.* pp.150-151.
49. Karl Marx and Frederick Engels, *The German Ideology*, Part I, (ed. C. J. Arthur), New York: International Publishers 1970, p.51.
50. Paulo Freire, *Education: The Practice of Freedom, op.cit.* p.48.
51. Paulo Freire, *Pedagogy of the Oppressed, op.cit.* pp.52-53.
52. Paulo Freire, 'Education, liberation and the church', *op.cit.* p.8.
53. Paulo Freire, *Pedagogy of the Oppressed, op.cit.* pp.35, 42, 52.
54. Paulo Freire, 'Education, liberation and the church', *op.cit.* p.2
55. *ibid.*
56. *ibid.*
57. Paulo Freire, *Pedagogy of the Oppressed, op.cit.* pp.53-54.
58. *ibid.* p.120.
59. *ibid.* pp.122, 131.
60. *ibid.* p.83.

61. *ibid.* p.164.
62. Paulo Freire, *Cultural Action for Freedom, op.cit.* p.74.
63. Paulo Freire, *Pedagogy of the Oppressed, op.cit.* pp.73-78.
64. *ibid.* p.124.
65. *ibid.* p.134.
66. *ibid.*
67. Alain Gheerbrant, *The Rebel Church in Latin America*, Penguin 1974, pp.349-350.
68. Paulo Freire, *Pedagogy of the Oppressed, op.cit.* p.41.
69. *ibid.* p.42.
70. See *Risk*, vol.II no.1, 1975, p.15.
71. Paulo Freire, *Pedagogy of the Oppressed, op.cit.* pp.131-132.
72. *ibid.* p.39.
73. *ibid.* p.76.
74. *ibid.* pp.75-77.
75. Paulo Freire, *Education: The Practice of Freedom, op.cit.* p.45.
76. Martin Buber, *Between Man and Man*, London: Fontana 1963, p.125.
77. Paulo Freire, *Pedagogy of the Oppressed, op.cit.* p.167.
78. *ibid.* p.63.
79. Paulo Freire, *Cultural Action for Freedom, op.cit.* pp.23-24.
80. Paulo Freire, *Pedagogy of the Oppressed, op.cit.* pp.70-71.
81. *ibid.* p.72.
82. Paulo Freire, *Cultural Action for Freedom, op.cit.* p.37.
83. Paulo Freire, 'Education, liberation and the church', *op.cit.* p.15.
84. Paulo Freire, *Cultural Action for Freedom, op.cit.* pp.17-18.

8. The End of Dialogue: Paulo Freire on Politics and Education

1. 'Controversial issues in secondary schools: Guidelines', a memorandum from the Director-General of Education to principals and teachers in New South Wales schools, Sydney 1976.
2. See: Paul Goodman, *Compulsory Miseducation:* New York: Vintage Books 1962; among Holt's many books *How Children Fail*, Penguin 1968, *The Underachieving School*, Penguin 1977, and *Instead of Education*, Penguin 1977; Jonathon Kozol, *Death at an Early Age*, Penguin 1968; Jules Henry, *Essays on Education*, Penguin 1974; George Dennison, *The Lives of Children*, New York: Vintage Books 1969; Ivan Illich, *Deschooling Society*, London: Calder and Boyars 1970; Everett Reimer, *School is Dead*, Penguin 1971.
3. Extreme in one sense only, that is within the tradition of remedying the evils of schooling by changing schooling itself: in this case abolishing it. Radical only if we assume that schooling itself is the basic source of the evils of schooling.
4. See: Illich, *op.cit.* p.viii; Reimer, *op.cit.* pp.167-8. But of most interest, see *Freire/Illich – The Oppression of Pedagogy and the Pedagogy of the Oppressed*, IDAC, World Council of Churches, Geneva, 1975.
5. The written output has been so vast and various that it would be pointless to attempt to list representative examples.
6. The attempt of Sam Bowles and Herb Gintis at a marxist political

156

economy of education is one of the clearest examples. 'We began our joint work in 1968 when, actively involved in campus political movements, and facing the mass of contradictory evidence on educational reform, we became committed to comprehensive intellectual reconstruction of the role of education in economic life.' S. Bowles and H. Gintis, *Schooling in Capitalist America*, New York: Basic Books 1976, pp.7-8.

7. Paulo Freire, 'Theology of liberation', in *Thinking with Paulo Freire*, a series of tapes available from the Australian Council of Churches, 199 Clarence Street, Sydney, NSW, Australia.

8. See: 'When I met Marx I continued to meet Christ on the corner of the street', in *The Age* newspaper, Melbourne, 19 April 1974.

9. I realise that to some extent this is a personal comment, and others will disagree with me. But compared to an encounter with Freire, the books do seem remarkably abstract. In theorising, abstraction more than anything else can override one's intentions, for example, by leading into idealistic interpretations of political struggle, something Freire does not intend.

10. See: Martin Carnoy, *Education as Cultural Imperialism*, New York: David McKay 1974.

11. Rosiska and Miguel Darcy de Oliveira, *Guinea-Bissau: Reinventing Education*, Geneva 1976. Although Freire is technically not the author of this document, it represents the work of the IDAC team, of which he is the chairman, and I shall quote it as if it represented his views, as I am sure he would wish. See also: Paulo Freire, *Pedagogy in Process: The Letters to Guinea-Bissau*, London: Writers and Readers Publishing Cooperative 1978; and O. Gjerstad and C. Sarrazin, *Sowing the First Harvest: National Reconstruction in Guinea-Bissau*, Oakland, California: Liberation Support Movement 1978.

12. Paulo Freire, *Pedagogy of the Oppressed*, Penguin 1972, p.31.

13. *ibid.*

14. Freire prefers the title 'Cultural action for liberation' instead of *Cultural Action for Freedom.*

15. *ibid.*

16. See William Minter, *Portuguese Africa and the West*, Penguin African Library 1972 – slightly out of date now, however. For very thorough treatment of African independence movements, see Basil Davidson, *In the Eye of the Storm: Angola's People*, Penguin African Library 1972, and especially Basil Davidson, Joe Slovo and Anthony R. Wilkinson, *Southern Africa: The New Politics of Revolution*, Penguin 1976. For a thorough discussion of political issues in Africa see A. Callinicos and J. Rogers, *Southern Africa after Soweto*, London: Pluto Press 1979.

17. Rosiska and Miguel Darcy de Oliveira, *Guinea-Bissau: Reinventing Education, op.cit.* p.19.

18. *ibid.*

19. *ibid.* pp.19-20.

20. Paulo Freire, *Pedagogy of the Oppressed, op.cit.* p.131.

21. Paulo Freire, 'Education, liberation and the church', in *Study Encounter*, vol.9 no.1, 1973, p.2.

22. See: Peter Berger, *Pyramids of Sacrifice*, Penguin 1974.

23. Amilcar Cabral, *Revolution in Guinea: An African People's Struggle*, London: Stage 1 1974, p.88. See also: Cabral, *Return to the Source: Selected*

Speeches of Amilcar Cabral, New York: Monthly Review Press with African Information Service, 1973.

24. *ibid.* pp.89-90.

25. Liberalism as an ideology (or interrelated ensemble of ideologies) is a very complex phenomenon, with varying strands taking forms according to the historical conjuncture obtaining. In very general terms, it represents the social world as basically an arena in which human wills and intentions can overcome material circumstances without being determined (by however complex a process) by the latter. Thus its fundamental values, such as 'freedom' (especially individual freedom) are reckoned realisable across various social and economic conditions, so long as they are underpinned by appropriate moral conceptions such as obligations and benevolence.

26. Karl Marx, 'Circular letter to Bebel, Liebknecht, Bracke, et.al.' in Karl Marx, *The First International and After*, Penguin 1974, p.375.

27. Paulo Freire, *Pedagogy of the Oppressed, op.cit.* pp.102-103.

28. In the present economic crisis, the depression of the wages of the middle class – or at least significant layers of it – is tending to push them towards a more proletarian position, and therefore potentially a radical consciousness. At the same time technological development makes many of their jobs (like workers' jobs) either redundant or subject to an increasing division of labour, in which case their actual conditions of work more and more closely resemble those of the factory. As examples, consider many clerical positions, computer programming, and some aspects of the work of teachers. For a very useful discussion of the question, see Harry Braverman, *Labor and Monopoly Capital: The Degradation of Work in the Twentieth Century*, New York: Monthly Review Press 1974, esp. Parts IV and V.

29. Paulo Freire, *Pedagogy of the Oppressed, op.cit.* p.118.

30. *ibid.* p.99.

31. *ibid.* p.102.

32. *ibid.* p.98.

33. Peter Berger claims that Freire's theory of humanisation, taken with the conscientisation idea, which Berger interprets as the raising of the consciousness of the oppressed by the intellectuals (an interpretation which unfortunately Freire is open to) means that Freire is not only an elitist in a rather vicious sense, but guilty of self-serving myopia. However, Berger's own perspective is so thoroughly idealist and abstract that he ignores the material reality of oppression altogether.

34. Paulo Freire, *Pedagogy of the Oppressed, op.cit.* p.139.

35. *ibid.* p.133.

36. *ibid.* pp.96-98.

37. *ibid.* pp.103-104.

38. *ibid.* p.41.

39. *ibid.* p.137.

40. *ibid.*

41. *ibid.*

42. Amilcar Cabral, *Revolution in Guinea: An African People's Struggle, op.cit.* p.88.

43. Paulo Freire, *Pedagogy of the Oppressed, op.cit.* p.106. Freire follows Mao straight down the line in his attempt to avoid seeming to place the leaders, educators or party in a position where they are actually teaching the

masses anything from a position of epistemic authority. See, for example, his quote from Mao: 'We must teach the masses clearly what we have received from them confusedly', on which Freire comments: 'This affirmation contains an entire dialogical theory of how to construct the programme content of education, which cannot be elaborated according to what the educator thinks best for his students.' (*ibid.* p.66) He cites Mao's injunction that the party wait patiently, and not make changes until the masses are on their side. As Mao says, 'Otherwise we shall isolate ourselves from the masses.' Indeed, Freire goes on 'There are two principles here: one is the actual needs of the masses rather than what we fancy they need, and the other is the wishes of the masses, who must make up their own minds instead of our making up their minds for them.' (*ibid.* p.67).

44. Amilcar Cabral, *Revolution in Guinea: An African People's Struggle,* *op.cit.* pp.48, 54-55.

45. That is, surplus value is extracted from the working class (exploitation) since there is no other way within the confines of the domestic economy to build up wealth (capital) necessary to provide the material basis for socialism. But since in the official ideology capitalism is not the prevailing mode of production, this is represented as the people having control. The control, however, can be exercised only through the party, which by definition, since it represents the will of the people and there is no class struggle between capitalists and proletariat, is the party of the people, and regards any independent organising as subversive of the people's interests, and hence represses it.

46. Rosiska and Miguel Darcy de Oliveira, *Guinea-Bissau: Reinventing Education, op.cit.* p.9.

47. Amilcar Cabral, *Revolution in Guinea: An African People's Struggle,* *op.cit.* pp.137-138.

48. Rosiska and Miguel Darcy de Oliveira, *Guinea-Bissau: Reinventing Education, op.cit.* p.34.

49. Amilcar Cabral, *Revolution in Guinea: An African People's Struggle, op.cit.* p.138.

50. Paulo Freire, *Pedagogy of the Oppressed, op.cit.* pp.129-130.

51. See: Alex Callincos and John Rogers, *Southern Africa After Soweto,* *op.cit.* and Nigel Harris, *The Mandate of Heaven: Marx and Mao in Modern China,* London: Quartet Books 1978.

Bibliography

Sources for Freire

A complete bibliography of Freire's writing has yet to be published. An extensive collection of sources can be found in Stanley M. Grabowski (ed.), *Paulo Freire: A Revolutionary Dilemma for the Adult Educator*, Syracuse New York: ERIC Clearing House on Adult Education 1972, pp.93-136, but this is now, obviously, a little out of date. More up to date information can be gained from Paulo Freire's office in Geneva. The address is 150 Route de Ferney, 1211, Geneva 20, Switzerland.

Books by Freire

Education for Critical Consciousness, London: Sheed and Ward 1974; republished as *Education: The Practice of Freedom*, London: Writers and Readers Publishing Cooperative 1976.

Pedagogy of the Oppressed, New York: The Continuum Publishing Company; and Penguin 1972.

Cultural Action for Freedom, Harvard Educational Review: Monograph no. 1, 1970, and Penguin 1972.

Pedagogy in Process: The Letters to Guinea-Bissau, New York: Seabury Press 1978; and London: Writers and Readers Publishing Cooperative 1978.

Articles and Papers by Freire

'Cultural Freedom in Latin America', in L. M. Colonese (ed.), *Human Rights and the Liberation of Man in the Americas*, Indiana: University of Notre Dame Press 1970.

'The Role of the Social Worker in the Process of Change', in *Sobre la Accion Cultural*, ICIRA, Chile 1970.

'The Political Literacy Process – An Introduction', Geneva: October 1970.

'Notes on Humanisation and its Educational Implications', a paper given to the seminar *Tomorrow Began Yesterday*, Rome: November 1970.

'Knowledge is a critical appraisal of the world', in *Ceres*, May-June 1971.

'A few notions about the word conscientisation', in *Hard Cheese*, no.1, 1971.

'Education for liberation or domestication', in *Perspectives*, vol.2 no.2, 1972.

'By learning they can teach', in *Convergence*, vol.6 no.1, 1973.

'Education, liberation and the church', in *Study Encounter*, vol.9 no.1, 1973.

'Political education experience in Peru', in *Tharunka*, 3 April 1974.

'Literacy and cultural invasion', in *The Open Book*, no.3, 1974.

'Research Methods', in *Literacy Discussion*, vol.5, 1974.

'Are adult literacy programmes neutral?', a paper given to the *International Symposium for Literacy*, Persepolis, September 1975.

'Pilgrims of the obvious', in *Risk*, vol.11, no.1, 1975.

Interviews with Freire

'Education for awareness', in *Risk*, vol.6 no.4, 1970, reprinted as chapter four in this volume.

'Conscientisation and liberation', Geneva: Institute for Cultural Action 1973.

Lister, I. 'Towards a pedagogy of the oppressed', in *The Times Higher Education Supplement*, 13 July 1973.

Shallcrass, J. 'The politics of education', in *New Zealand Listener*, 13 April 1974.

Hill, B. 'When I met Marx I continued to meet Christ on the corners of the street', in *The Age* newspaper, Melbourne, 19 April 1974.

'*Thinking with Paulo Freire*', a series of tapes made during Freire's visit to Australia in 1974, and available from the Australian Council of Churches, 199 Clarence Street, Sydney, NSW, Australia.

Commentaries on Freire

Berger, P. *Pyramids of Sacrifice*, Penguin 1977.

Bourne, R. 'Alternatives to school', in C. Harding and C. Roper (eds.), *Latin American Review of Books 1*, California: Ramparts Press 1973.

Bowers, C. A. *Cultural Literacy for Freedom*, New York: Elan Books 1974.

Demaine, J. 'On the new sociology of education', in *Economy and Society*, vol.6 no.2, 1977.

de Oliveira, R. and Dominice, P. *Freire: Illich*, Geneva: Institute for Cultural Action 1974.

Eastman, G. 'Freire, Illich and revolutionary pedagogy', in *Dialogue*, vol.6 no.1, 1972.

Elias, J. L., *Conscientisation and Deschooling*, Philadelphia: The Westminister Press 1977.

Egerton, J. 'Searching for Freire', in *Saturday Review of Education*, vol.1, no.3, 1973.

Epstein, E. H. 'The social control thesis and educational reform in dependent nations', in *Theory and Society*, vol.5 no.2, May 1978.

Fonseca, C. 'Paulo Freire in Bombay', in *New Frontiers in Education*, vol.3 no.2, 1973.

Gleeson, D. 'Theory and practice in the sociology of Paulo Freire', in *Universities Quarterly*, vol.28 no.3, 1974.

Grabowski, S. M. (ed.) *Paulo Freire: A Revolutionary Dilemma for the Adult Educator*, Syracuse New York: ERIC Clearing House on Adult Education 1972.

Halley, C. 'Paulo Freire – personal impressions', in *Dialogue*, vol.7 no.1, 1973.

Haviland, R. M. 'An introduction to the writings of Paulo Freire', in *Adult Education*, vol.45 no.5, 1973.

Hodges, P. 'A voice in the silence', in *The New Internationalist*, August 1977.

Ireland, R. 'Paulo Freire in context', in *Dialogue*, vol.6 no.2, 1972.

Lloyd, A. S., 'Paulo Freire and conscientisation', in *Adult Education*, vol.23 no.1, 1972.

Lovell, D. 'Paulo Freire at Belgrave' in *Dialogue*, vol. 8, no.2, 1974.

Mackie, R. 'Freire, revolution and education', in *Radical Education Dossier*, no.2, March 1977.

Murphy, J. 'Paulo Freire's programme for adult literacy', in *The Forum of Education*, vol.36, no.3, 1977.

Musgrave, P. and Selleck, R. J. *Alternative Schools*, Sydney: John Wiley 1975.

Nasan, D. 'Reconsidering Freire', in *Liberation*, vol.18 no.10, 1974.

Reynolds, J. and Skilbeck, M. *Culture and the Classroom*, London: Macmillan 1976.

Sanders, T. G. 'The educational method of Paulo Freire', in *Dissent*, no.30, Spring 1973.

Sanders, T. G. 'The Paulo Freire method – literacy training and conscientisation', in *Dialogue*, vol.7 no.1, 1973.

Sanders, T. G. 'Paulo Freire: his method', in *Cold Comfort*, vol.3 no.1, April 1974.

Selleck, R. J. 'Paulo Freire and manipulation', in *Dialogue*, vol.6 no.3, 1972.

Spring, J. *A Primer of Libertarian Education*, New York: Free Life Editions 1975.

Stanley, M. 'Literacy: The crisis of a conventional wisdom', in *Convergence*, vol.6 no.1, 1973.

Wright, C. and J. 'Paulo Freire – Report of a personal encounter', in *Dialogue*, vol.7 no.1, 1973.

Wright, C. 'Paulo Freire – What is the importance of his pedagogy for Australia?' in *Cold Comfort*, vol.3 no.1, April 1974.

Latin American Background

Arraes, M. *Brazil: The People and the Power*, Penguin 1972.

Bowles, S. 'Cuban education and the revolutionary ideology', in *Harvard Educational Review*, vol.41 no.4 1971.

Buchanan, K. *Reflections on Education in the Third World*, Nottingham: Spokesman Books 1975.

Carnoy, M. *Education as Cultural Imperialism*, David McKay: New York 1975.

Debray, R. *Revolution in the Revolution?* Penguin 1968.

de Castro, J. *Death in the North-East*, New York: Vintage Books 1969.

de Kadt, E. *Catholic Radicals in Brazil*, London: Oxford University Press 1970.

Evans, P. 'Continuities and contradictions in the evolution of Brazilian dependence', in *Latin American Perspectives*, vol.3 no.2, 1976.

Flynn, P. 'The Military Decade', in *Current Affairs Bulletin*, 1 July 1974.

Frank, A. G. *Capitalism and Underdevelopment in Latin America*, New York: Monthly Review Press 1967.

Gerassi, J. (ed.) *Venceremos! The Speeches and Writings of Che Guevara*, New York: Simon and Schuster 1968.

Guevara, E. *Guerrilla Warfare*, Penguin 1969.

Harding, C. and Roper, C. (eds.) *Latin American Review of Books I*, Palo Alto: Ramparts Press 1973.

Heimer, F. W. 'Education and politics in Brazil', in *Comparative Education Review*, February 1975.

Horowitz, I. L. (ed.) *Masses in Latin America*, New York: Oxford University Press 1970.

Julias, F. *Cambao – The Yoke*, Penguin 1972.

Marighela, C. *For the Liberation of Brazil*, Penguin 1971.

Niedergang, M. *The Twenty Latin Americas*, vols.I, II, Penguin 1971.

Quartim, J. *Dictatorship and Armed Struggle in Brazil*, London: New Left Books 1971.

Skidmore, T. E. *Politics in Brazil: 1930-64*, London: Oxford University Press 1969.

Wheelwright, E. L. *Radical Political Economy*, Sydney: ANZ Books 1974.

African Background

Cabral, A. *Return to the Source: Selected Speeches of Amilcar Cabral*, New York: Monthly Review Press 1973.

Cabral, A. *Revolution in Guinea: An African People's Struggle*, London: Stage I 1974.

Callinicos, A. and Rogers, J. *Southern Africa after Soweto*, London: Pluto Press 1977.

Davidson, B. *The Liberation of Guinea*, Penguin 1969.

Davidson, B. *In the Eye of the Storm: Angola's People*, Penguin 1972.

164

Davidson, B., Slovo, J. and Wilkinson, A. R. *Southern Africa: The New Politics of Revolution*, Penguin 1976.

de Oliveira, R. and M. *Guinea-Bissau: Reinventing Education*, Geneva: Institute for Cultural Action 1976.

Gjerstad, O. and Sarrazin, C. *Sowing the First Harvest: National Reconstruction in Guinea-Bissau*, Oakland: Liberation Support Movement 1978.

Fanon, F. *The Wretched of the Earth*, Penguin 1967.

Memmi, A. *The Colonizer and the Colonized*, New York: Orion Press 1965.

Mintner, W. *Portuguese Africa and the West*, Penguin 1972.

Freire's Literacy Process: Related Works

Ashton-Warner, S. *Teacher*, New York: Simon and Schuster 1963.

Berggren, C. and L. *The Literacy Process: A Practice in Domestication or Liberation*, London: Writers and Readers Publishing Cooperative 1975.

Brown, C. 'Literacy in thirty hours: Paulo Freire's process', in *Urban Review*, vol.7 no.3, July 1974.

Brown, C. *Literacy in Thirty Hours: Paulo Freire's Literacy Process in North-East Brazil*, London: Writers and Readers Publishing Cooperative 1975.

Bughee, J. 'The Freire approach to literacy: Review and reflections', in *Literacy Discussion*, vol.4 no.4, 1973.

Hoyles, M. (ed.) *The Politics of Literacy*, London: Writers and Readers Publishing Cooperative 1977.

Philosophical and Intellectual Background to Freire

Althusser, L. *For Marx*, London: Allen Lane the Penguin Press 1969.

Buber, M. *I and Thou*, second edition, Edinburgh: T. and T. Clark 1959.

Buber, M. *Between Man and Man*, London: Fontana 1961.

Fromm, E. *Fear of Freedom*, London: Routledge and Kegan Paul 1960.

Fromm, E. *Marx's Concept of Man*, New York: Frederick Ungar 1961.

Fromm, E. (ed.) *Socialist Humanism*, New York: Doubleday 1965.

Fromm, E. *The Heart of Man*, London: Routledge and Kegan Paul 1966.

Garaudy, R. *From Anathema to Dialogue*, London: Collins 1967.

Garaudy, R. *The Alternative Future*, Penguin 1976.

Gerassi, J. *Revolutionary Priest: The Complete Writings and Messages of Camillo Torres*, New York: Random House 1971.

Gheebrant, A. *The Rebel Church in Latin America*, Penguin 1974.

Girardi, G. *Marxism and Christianity*, Dublin: Gill and Son 1968.

Gramsci, A. *Selections from the Prison Notebooks*, London: Lawrence and Wishart 1971.

Gutierrez, G. A. *A Theology of Liberation*, New York: Orbis Books 1973.

Hebblethwaite, P. *The Christian-Marxist Dialogue and Beyond*, London: Darton, Longman and Todd 1977.

Kolakowski, L. *Towards a Marxist Humanism*, New York: Grove Press 1968.

Lenin, V. I. *What is to be Done?* London: Panther 1970.

Lukacs, G. *History and Class Consciousness*, London: Merlin Books 1971.

Mao Tse-tung, *Four Essays on Philosophy*, Peking: Foreign Languages Press 1968.

Marcel, G. *Man Against Mass Society*, New York: Regnery Gate 1962.

Marx, K. *Early Writings*, Penguin 1975.

Marx, K. *Surveys from Exile*, Penguin 1973.

Marx, K. *The Revolutions of 1848*, Penguin 1973.

Marx, K. *Capital*, Vol.I, Penguin 1976.

Marx, K. and Engels F. *The German Ideology*, (C. J. Arthur ed.), New York: International Publishers 1970.

Niebuhr, R. *Moral Man and Immoral Society*, New York: Scribners 1960.

Popper, K. *The Open Society and Its Enemies*, vols.I and II, London: Routledge and Kegan Paul 1962.

Sartre, J. P. *Search for a Method*, New York: Vintage Books 1968.

Sartre, J. P. *Between Existentialism and Marxism*, London: New Left Books 1974.